101 SMART QUESTIONS TO ASK on Your INTERVIEW

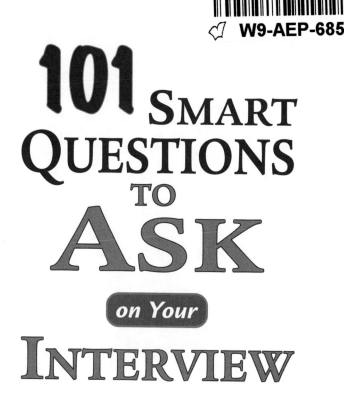

Join us on the web at

careersuccess.delmar.com

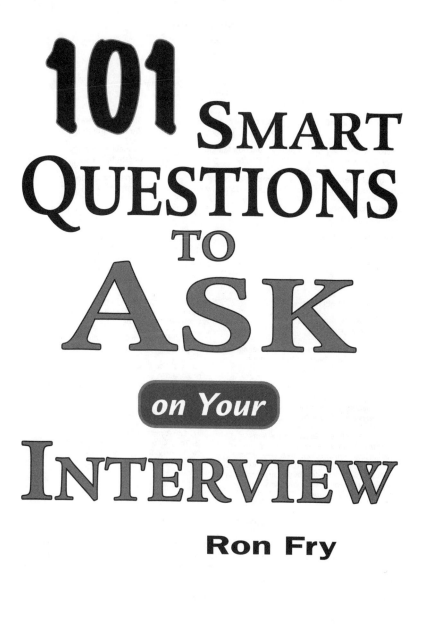

101 SMART QUESTIONS TO ASK on Your INTERVIEW

Ron Fry

THOMSON

DELMAR LEARNING

Australia Brazil Canada Mexico Singapore Spain United Kingdom United States

THOMSON

DELMAR LEARNING

101 Smart Questions to Ask on Your Interview
Ron Fry

Vice President, Career Education SBU: Dawn Gerrain

Director of Learning Solutions: Sherry Dickinson

Managing Editor: Robert L. Serenka, Jr.

Acquisitions Editor: Martine Edwards

Developmental Editor: Jennifer Anderson

Editorial Assistant: Falon Ferraro

Director of Production: Wendy A. Troeger

Production Manager: J.P. Henkel

Production Editor: Rebecca Goldthwaite

Director of Marketing: Wendy E. Mapstone

Channel Manager: Gerard McAvey

Marketing Specialist: Erica Conley

For permission to use material from this text or product, submit a request online at http://www.thomsonrights.com

Any additional questions about permissions can be submitted by email to thomsonrights@thomson.com

Library of Congress Cataloging-in-Publication Data
Fry, Ronald W.
    101 smart questions to ask on your interview / Ron Fry.—2nd ed.
        p. cm.
    ISBN-13: 978-1-4180-4001-7
    ISBN-10: 1-4180-4001-0
    1. Employment interviewing.
    I. Title: One-hundred-and-one smart questions to ask on your interview. II. Title.
    HF5549.5.I6F757 2006
    650.14′4—dc22
                                                            2006007992

NOTICE TO THE READER

CONTENTS

INTRODUCTION

How To Be A Great Prospect

"Today's economy requires job hunters to be more proactive, more sophisticated, and more willing to go through brick walls to get what they want. Employers no longer plan your career for you. You must look after yourself, and know what you want and how to get it."

KATE WENDLETON, *INTERVIEWING AND SALARY NEGOTIATION*

Most job candidates think of the interview in completely the wrong way. They think of it as an interrogation, a police lineup. And they see themselves as suspects, not as the key prospects they really are.

This book will show you that you are, to a very large degree, *in charge of the interview.* It will convince you that you are there not only to sell the company on *you,* but to make sure that *you* are sold on *them.* It will give you the powerful questions that will work whatever your age, whatever your experience, whatever your goals.

It will *not,* however, spend very much time preparing you for the questions the interviewer is going to throw at *you.* Luckily for you (why am I so good to you?), I've already written the companion book to this one—*101 Great Answers to the Toughest Interview Questions*—whose sole purpose is to do exactly that. (Not only did I already write it, I've already revised it four times, and it's already sold well over a million copies.) Using these two books together, you will be amply armed for any interview and any interviewer.

Even though I think you should buy a copy of my other book, I am going to reveal a secret that may cost me sales: There really aren't 101 questions you have to prepare yourself for. Not even a dozen. There are only five questions interviewers desperately want to know your answers to:

Can you do the job?

Do you have the specific qualifications I'm seeking? Do you have the right degree? The right experience? The appropriate skills?

Will you do the job . . .

. . . better than the other people I'm interviewing? Prove to me that you're the best person for the job.

Will you actually *take* the job if I offer it to you?

How hungry are you? How much do you actually want *this* specific job? Or are you so desperate you'll take *any* job . . . even this one?

Even if you are perfectly qualified and highly motivated, do I think you will fit in with the rest of the group?

The smaller the company or department, the more important this chemistry question becomes. In a one- or two-person office, it may be the *key* question.

Will you make me, the interviewer, look like a genius for recommending or hiring you?

Or will your miscues and missteps make me look like an idiot, kill my promotion, slash my bonus, maybe even jeopardize my own job? (The higher up on the food chain the interviewer is, the more central this question becomes to her.)

Will you ever be asked these questions? Probably not. You will be asked dozens of questions about your strengths and weaknesses, your successes and failures, your plans and ideas. Just remember: The answers to *these* five questions is what all the *other* questions are really trying to ascertain.

WHY ASK QUESTIONS?

Crafting concise, targeted, enthusiastic, and positive responses to the interviewer's questions gives you an opportunity to demonstrate your knowledge of the company and industry and show how your qualifications would help you fit right in. *Asking* concise, targeted, and well-crafted questions gives you additional chances to demonstrate the extent of your research, to build on whatever rapport you've established, and to align what you know and can do with what the company needs.

These questions, by their very nature, proclaim that *you are interested*. Likewise, the complete *lack* of questions will undoubtedly convince most interviewers that you are *not* interested.

Oh, you *were* interested? You just didn't *have* any questions. Sorry, interviewers don't consider that an option. No questions? No job offer. That's certainly a rule with a vast majority of interviewers. (No, no, please, don't try the "but the interviewer was so good that he answered all my questions" bit. Doesn't work. Wouldn't be prudent. Not going to go there.)

As I'm going to emphasize throughout this book, asking questions the smart way is just another way to match your skills, talents, and qualifications to the company's needs; it's another opportunity to demonstrate that you are far and away the only candidate the interviewer should consider. By preceding many of your questions with a phrase or statement that reminds the interviewer of something you said earlier or a point you want to continually reemphasize, it's another chance to "blow your own horn":

> *"Mr. Jones, as my stint at Eubonics, Inc. clearly showed, I have the ability to motivate a team to overachieve, but could you tell me a little more about the individuals I'd be working with here?"*

HOW TO CONSTRUCT SMART QUESTIONS

Let me save the obsessive-compulsives among you some time— there are far more than 101 smart questions in this book. How do I know (because *I* didn't count them!)? While there may be 101 general questions in the book (although I *think* there are quite a few more), there are a near-infinite number of specific, qualifying, clarifying questions you can ask. I intend to point you in the right direction, but the details of such questions are going to be determined by your exact situation, by what you've already said during the interview, and by what the interviewer has already said. How much (or little) research you've done will also expand (or limit) the depth and breadth of your questions.

Here's an example of how to construct dozens of great questions after asking a general question and receiving a relatively innocuous reply from the interviewer:

> **You:** *"Mr. Barton, I noticed in the latest issue of* **Publisher's Weekly** *that you intend to increase the number of books you publish next year from 50 to 72."*

Him: *"Yes, we do."* (Hmmm, lot of detail there, really something to grab onto. Would it have killed him to give you *some*thing more to go on?)

Here are just *some* of the questions that would naturally evolve from this initial exchange:

Why did you make that decision?

Who made that decision?

Do you know what categories the additional books will be published in?

How did you settle on 22 additional books?

Are you going to publish in categories other than your traditional ones?

Do you have a feel for the kinds of new books you're seeking?

How would that expansion affect my position? My department? My superior? My subordinates?

Is my position being created in whole or in part because of that decision?

Will others have to be hired as well? In what departments?

Does this mean the company believes the market for printed books will continue to expand?

What is the mix of the new books, in terms of fiction versus nonfiction, hardcover versus paperback?

Is the company able to fund this expansion without going to the capital markets?

I could go on and on. And, in fact, to every answer Mr. Barton gives to each of the above questions, *another* half dozen questions should easily spring to mind. Follow-up questions are the heart and soul of the interview process . . . *from both sides of the desk.*

While I'll be talking much more about how to phrase follow-up questions in the chapters to come, let me point out one thing our hypothetical candidate did in a couple of the above questions: She *assumed the position.* In other words, she referred to "*my* department," "*my* superiors," and "*my* position," *implying that the job was already hers.* Such a subtle strategy may have no effect if she is otherwise unqualified for the job, but it *may* turn out to be the "tipping point" if she winds up neck-and-neck with another candidate.

SO, DO YOU HAVE ANY QUESTIONS?

Normally, this question occurs very near the conclusion of the interview. In fact, you may well assume that its appearance signals that end.

But do you have to wait until the interviewer puts you through the wringer, smiles benevolently, and actually asks if you have any questions? I really don't think so, but there are a couple of caveats to keep in mind before you charge ahead doing your best Barbara Walters impression.

Always request permission to ask the first couple of questions. Once it's clear the interviewer has no problem with *you* asking questions, even as she continues to pepper you with her own, you will have established a flow and won't need to ask permission each time. But it's up to you to make sure the interviewer is comfortable with your approach. If he shows obvious signs of discomfort—frowning while saying "Okay," pursing his lips, or showing in any other way that he is *not* too keen on your interrupting his supposedly well-crafted approach to the interview session—back off!

But if an interviewer suggests you are free to ask questions at any time or tells you it's fine when you request permission, do so! In that case, waiting for the ubiquitous "Do you have any questions?" is a bad move: The interviewer may have already downgraded you because you *didn't* take her (strong) hint to be assertive right from the start.

Asking questions during the regular interview does not mean interrupting. And it doesn't mean always answering an interviewer's question with a question of your own, which may well thwart the interviewer's attempts to assess your strengths. (And you don't want to thwart him, do you?)

Taking the initiative and asking questions early (with the interviewer's permission, of course) is the scenario I prefer, both as an interviewee and an interviewer.

As an interviewer, it impresses me. It makes me believe (barring evidence to the contrary) that the person in front of me is interested, engaged, and assertive.

As an interviewee, I want to control the interview, and asking questions early and often certainly accomplishes that. Doing so is especially effective with an inept (or less-than-veteran) interviewer, who may welcome your help!

Another great reason to ask questions early and often is because it transforms a stilted, traditional "Q & A" session—with you being the "A"—into a *conversation*. By definition, this makes the meeting less formal, less "you versus me," more "we." And a conversation is how you explore areas of common interest, trade comments, and chat rather than "talk." In other words, the way you establish the chemistry that is one of the vital factors in landing any job!

Last but not least, asking a good question is a slick way to sidestep an uncomfortable question from the interviewer (at least for the time being). What's the story with that one-year gap in your resume? Darn. You didn't want to have to talk about that aborted dot-com bomb *yet*. Don't expect the topic to die. You are probably just buying a temporary reprieve, but at least you've given yourself a little time to think about how you want to defuse it.

HOW TO USE THIS BOOK

It's as important to know how and when to ask a question as it is to know what questions to ask. In Chapter 1, we'll talk about questioning strategy—general rules to follow to ensure your questions are concise, appropriate, timely, and to-the-point. Oh, and that they actually accomplish what you want them to.

Chapter 2 is, in my mind, the most important in the book, even though it has nothing to do with questions to ask on your interview. Rather, it details questions to ask *yourself* before you even make a phone call, answer an ad, meet with a recruiter, or send out a resume. It won't do you much good to have a list of fantastic questions to ask an interviewer if you're seeking the wrong job at the wrong company in the wrong industry! Chapter 2 will ensure you take the time to analyze who you are, what's important to you, and what you ideally want in a job and a career.

Once you know where you're going, Chapter 3 will give you the help you need to begin researching the companies you intend to target.

In Chapter 4, you'll start constructing the smart questions to ask "preinterviewers"—employment agencies, recruiters, headhunters, and Human Resources—who can't say "yes" but can certainly say "no"!

In Chapters 5, 6, and 7, you'll be ready to finally concentrate on the questions to ask the hiring manager—the person who can actually say those magic words, "You're hired! When can you start?"

Chapter 5 covers basic questions about the company, department, and job; "probing" questions designed to elicit more and more detail; "style" questions about your potential boss and the corporate culture; and "preclosing" questions to get a better feel for how the interview is going and what you need to do to land the job.

In Chapter 6, I give you a series of great "closing" questions to help you identify hidden objections, find out about the other candidates (your competition), and push for an offer.

Finally, in Chapter 7, I'll tell you what to do when you actually receive a job offer and how to get the best deal—when and how to discuss salary, bonuses, benefits, and perks, and how to maximize your compensation package. I'll also discuss how to handle the rejections endemic to the job-search process.

Just remember, like playing the piano, interviewing takes practice, and practice makes perfect. My own hours of personal interviewing experience—the tragedies and the triumphs—as well as my years as an interviewer, are the basis for this book. I hope to spare you many of the indignities I suffered along the way by preparing you for the interview of your worst nightmares—at a comfortable remove from the interviewer's glare.

Enough preparation. Let's get busy.

CHAPTER

When, Where, Why, and How to Ask Smart Questions

Before we start delving into specific questions to ask yourself, let's agree on some overarching rules, if you will, that will govern them.

SHAPE YOUR QUESTIONS TO THE POSITION

Learn as much as you can about the position for which you're interviewing—*before* you show up for *any* interview. When you ask questions about any aspect of the industry, company, department, or job, make sure they are couched in terms of the requirements of the specific job you're seeking and the goals of the particular company at which you hope to be hired.

DON'T ASK ABOUT TIME OFF

Or vacations or sick days or anything other than the job at hand . . . at least not until you're *offered* the job.

DON'T ASK ABOUT SALARY OR BENEFITS

Again, wait until you are offered the job. (See chapter 7 to understand why.) You don't want money to be a factor if the interviewer is still wondering whether you're the best person for the job . . . or even worthy of a callback.

KNOW WHAT TO ASK WHEN OF WHOM

Questions differ depending on both where you are in the interviewing process (screening, hiring, first, second, or third interview, etc.) and, during a particular interview, where you are in the interviewer's script.

The earlier you are in the process, the more likely you'll be asking general questions about where the company's going, its culture, and what it deems important or valuable. Your questions are an attempt to get an initial feel for how you'd fit in, where you'd fit in, whether and how you could grow, and so on.

The more time you devote to a particular company, the more targeted and probing the questions should become, both those the interviewer asks you and those you ask the interviewer. You'll really want to start honing in on the particular information you need to decide whether this is the right company, position, and boss for you. So the farther along in the process, the more individualized the questions become (since what's most important to you may be something I wouldn't even ask about, like the availability of on-site daycare, reimbursement of moving expenses, or tuition).

GET THE INTERVIEWER TALKING

Ask open-ended questions—those that begin with "Who," "What," "When," "Where," or "How." Your purpose is to establish a conversation, to get the interviewer talking so he volunteers the information you want (and, just maybe, to elicit some information you don't even *know* you want). These kinds of questions do that. Closed-ended questions—those that can be answered by a simple "yes" or "no" (and undoubtedly will be)—are useful near the end of an interview, when you want to close the sale or when you *do* want specific answers to specific questions. *"Do I have to wait 90 days for medical coverage?"* A simple "yes" or "no" will suffice.

"Why" questions can be a little tricky, since if you're not sensitive (or aware), they can make you come off as overly aggressive: *"I noticed you put a lot of books out of print last year. Why did you do that?"*

You can extract the same information in a gentler way: *"It seems from your annual report that more books than usual were remaindered last year. Was that mainly the effect of 9/11?"*

Ask probing, open-ended questions to extract more details and to follow up after general questions.

Consider asking questions that *aren't* questions. Making a statement rather than asking pointed queries is a way to put a nervous interviewer at ease. It takes some practice, but it's very effective in getting reluctant interviewers to open up: *"What would help me most would be to get a better feel for the culture I'd be walking into and the styles of the people with whom I'd be working. Could you take a couple of minutes to give me a better understanding of those issues?"*

MATCH YOUR STYLE TO THE INTERVIEWER'S STYLE

This doesn't mean you have to become a total milquetoast when interviewing with a passive interviewer, but, when facing such a person, it may behoove you to tone down the "sales killer" personality a bit.

That's why you have to be a little careful about a one-size-fits-all interview approach. Yes, employers want confident candidates and hard workers. But take the time to look around whatever office you're visiting. Is everyone pretty laid back? Then don't come on like a house afire! You can crow about the results you achieved without scaring everyone.

Likewise, if you're inherently reluctant to blow your own horn anyway and a little passive and laid back yourself, an atmosphere akin to a penny stock boiler room might not be your cup of tea, even if they *are* looking for a "detail-oriented accountant type."

WATCH THE INTERVIEWER'S BODY LANGUAGE

You also need to gauge the interviewer's response to what you're saying, not just the answers you've given but the questions you've asked. Listen for verbal clues and watch for body language that will often tell you how you're *really* doing. If it's obvious you've hit a wrong note, you may even want to say something like, *"I'm sorry. That question seemed to make you uncomfortable. Is that an area you're not yet prepared to talk about?"* Again, you don't want to kill a potential job because you were overly aggressive during the interview.

If you know what to look for, you'll get extra clues from the body language of an interviewer:

- **Lack of eye contact** or shifting eyes are usually seen as a sign of dishonesty or, at best, discomfort: *"Mr. Interviewer, are you planning any more layoffs?"* [squint, shift, shift, shift . . .] *"Uh, no, Jim. So, how about dem Bears?"*

- **Raised eyebrows** indicate disbelief or even mild distain, along the lines of *"Oh, really?"* / *"You don't mean that, do you?"* / *"Gee, how'd you figure that out?* / *"You don't actually expect me to buy that, do you?"*

- **A smile at the wrong time** can be a sign of discomfort or an indication of a complete lack of appropriate social skills!

- **"Closed" positions of the hands and arms**—clenched fists, arms folded across the body—are not positive. They may also indicate boredom or negativity.

- An interviewer who is **slumping** or leaning back in his chair may be showing disrespect (arrogance) or disinterest. It is surely a sign that you have to ask a question to get him back into the conversation and his head back to your candidacy.

- Doodling, chewing on a pencil, scratching, playing with one's hands, moving things around on a desk, or acting distracted are typical **signs of nervousness.** Don't interpret such signs as anything *more* than nerves unless something else tips you off. Again, ask a question to get the focus back on you or, even better, a question about *them*—everyone likes to talk about themselves (especially a not-too-experienced interviewer who seems to be nervous about interviewing *you,* believe it or not!).

BE CONCISE AND TO THE POINT

If your question is so long that even *you* don't remember the beginning by the time you finally reach the end, what do you expect the poor interviewer to do? Ask one question at a time, not a series of questions masquerading as a multi-clause construction. Then follow up with some equally pointed and specific questions to elicit more information.

ASSUME THE POSITION

Even when my brother, Ken, was a relatively low-level salesperson at his previous company, he constantly talked about what "we" were doing and how "we" were doing it and what "our" prospects were. Despite the fact that he was not privy to the executive ranks until late in his tenure—what "they" knew or where "they" were headed—his use of "we" certainly gave the impression he was more involved in those decisions than he was . . . and he wasn't involved at all in any of them!

It must have worked. His last title there was President of Sales.

Learn from my bro. When appropriate, assume you already have the job and ask questions accordingly: *"Mr. Baines, what's the first challenge we're going to face together?" "Ms. Lyndon, what projections do we need to hit next year?" "Mr. Johnson, what are the three most important targets you have for my department?"*

DON'T ASK QUESTIONS THAT SHOW YOUR IGNORANCE . . .

. . . or your lack of good research, poor sense of taste, or strange sense of humor. And don't ask questions that are just plain wacko:

> *"Does it matter that I majored in religion?"*

> *"Who named the company?"*

> *"Do you think Puerto Rico should become the 51st state?"*

> *"Should I tweeze my eyebrows?"*

DON'T ASK QUESTIONS THAT REVEAL YOUR BIASES

"Hmm, Rutigliano, that's Italian, isn't it?"

"Will I be working with a lot of people babbling in another language?"

"Will my boss have any trouble following my directions? After all, I did graduate first in my class at MIT, and I understand he barely made it through Jimmy Dean's School of Air Conditioning and Sausage-making."

DON'T MAKE AN INTERVIEWER OBVIOUSLY UNCOMFORTABLE . . .

. . . by asking questions like the biased, ignorant, or just plain weird ones above, or those that are too personal (*"Tell me about your children." "Are you married?"*); too desperate (*"I really need to pay the rent by next Friday. If you offer me this job, could I get a loan before I start?"*); or too incredibly arrogant (*"I have a few problems with the offer. Since you can't seem to do anything about it, may I talk to someone with the authority to give me what I want?"*).

And avoid any question that has little or nothing to do with the job, department, or company. These may include, but are not limited to, asking for a date, inquiring about the smoking-break policy, or asking any question that would lead even the most understanding interviewer to immediately call security and have you forcibly ejected, preferably from the state.

DON'T INTRODUCE NEGATIVITY INTO AN INTERVIEWER'S MIND

There is nothing inherently wrong with asking about normal work hours, as long as you don't say, *"My last boss expected me to work most Saturdays. You don't, do you?"* Oh, yeah, you are *so* committed.

As I've noted, some questions are inappropriate only when asked at the wrong time. When you have been offered a job, it is expected that you will want to know everything about your proposed compensation, vacation schedules, holidays, and all that other practical stuff. But asking about vacation days in the first five minutes of an interview is not recommended.

DON'T TELL A JOKE . . .

. . . even if you think you're the next Chris Rock.

Most of us think we're a lot funnier than we actually are, and humor is, to murder a metaphor, in the ear of the beholder. Why take a chance that some lame joke may cost you a job? Be at ease, feel free to smile and even offer a humorous (or at least less than serious) comment if it seems in keeping with the rest of the conversation. But please remember that you are there to convince them to hire you and assess whether you want to be hired, not to audition for a gig at the Laff Factory.

NEVER LET THEM SEE YOU SWEAT

Don't ask questions that make you appear desperate . . . even if you've been terminated from your previous job!

I noticed something truly bizarre during my dating days. When I was young and single and HUNGRY, I seemed to give off vibes that screamed, *"Warning! Warning! Women beware. Desperate bachelor on the prowl."* Not long after I got married, I was out with friends and seemed to suddenly be a rock star. Virtually every single woman in the bar was smiling at me, sending over a drink, making it obvious that she was interested.

What the heck was happening? I was never a lady killer, and my (okay, not great) looks hadn't suddenly changed. George Clooney didn't need to worry about me scarfing up all the available women. Well, my totally unscientific, amateur, unsupported premise is that the same vibes that had cried desperation were now sending out soothing, happy, contented signals . . . and people were responding the way you would expect them to.

Interviewers, whether men or women, will react in the same way. Be desperate, think desperate, and you might as well walk in carrying a sign saying "Will work for anyone, do anything, require nothing." That is not the message employers want to hear and, I suspect, not the one you want to be sending them.

This is also a factor when you are trying to find a job, *any* job, and are clearly overqualified for the ones you're pursuing. It's hard to feign interest in a job you don't really care about. Did you pick a "safety" college when you were a high school senior, one you figured you'd have no problem getting into if the places you *really* wanted to go turned you down? Did any of you get *rejected* by your safety schools? Maybe when you interviewed there, you unconsciously sent them the message that they *were* your safety schools! No employer wants someone who "just wants a job, any job."

REMEMBER IT'S A TWO-WAY STREET

It's impossible to lead you by the hand through a whole series of potential questions—smart or not—for the simple reason that the specific questions you choose to ask should be an attempt to redefine the job so it more closely fits your qualifications. Let me explain.

In very large companies, job titles and descriptions seem to be etched in stone. But the smaller the company, the more likely there are a plethora of possible duties, not all of which any single person can do. Or not all of which any single person is qualified to do. So, especially at the smaller company (but even at many of the larger ones), you'll want to attempt to customize the job the employer *thinks* he is offering you so it more closely matches the qualifications you have.

Let me give you an example of how this can work. My publishing company, Career Press, has seven editors. One is exclusively acquisitions, meaning he finds the books that the company is going to publish each season (or, at least, develops a solid list from which to choose). The other six are involved in production, everything from working with authors on their manuscripts in a general way (suggesting they move a chapter, kill an example, add a checklist, and so on) to detailed line editing, proofreading, designing the interior "look," to then executing that format and getting the book off to the printer.

Not long ago, we needed to hire a new editor. My Editor-in-chief wanted another "word" person who could do initial editing on every manuscript that came in, then pass each off to an editor who would work with the author on the more detailed, line-by-line edits.

But then Jinny walked in and declared, *"Look, I can't really edit in a general way. In fact, I'm not really that kind of editor at all. But I am the best darn formatter you ever saw. Instead of hiring a general editor, why don't you let the rest of the editors spend more time editing and I'll spend all my time designing their books, laying them out, and getting them off to the printer?"*

If this happened anywhere else, especially a large publishing house like Random House or Simon & Schuster, the Editor-in-chief probably would have said, *"Thanks, but no thanks."* But some smaller houses (like Career Press) probably would have taken the time to consider such a change in plans.

Jinny, who was not *remotely* qualified for the opening as it was described and advertised, gave herself a chance to actually get a job by encouraging the editor to *redefine the job so it fit her qualifications.*

In actual fact, it worked. She is a great employee!

IT'S OKAY TO BE A COPYCAT

Feel free to take some of the typical interview questions *you* should expect to be asked and ask them of the interviewer instead:

> **What are the company's (department's) strengths and weaknesses?**
>
> **What was the last great challenge faced by the department? How did you and your team handle it?**
>
> **Can you tell me about a successful project and how you managed it?**
>
> **Can you tell me about some recent problems you've faced and how you (as a team) overcame them?**
>
> **What's your definition of success? What's your definition of failure?**
>
> **If you could change one thing about the way this department works (or is structured or is managed or is compensated), what would it be?**
>
> **How often do you and your team socialize outside of work? Is such extracurricular activity actively promoted? Tolerated? Discouraged?**

ASK FOR THE JOB IF YOU WANT IT

The more sales-oriented the job—the more Type A the inter-viewer or the observed company culture—the more aggres-sively you need to close the sale. In fact, lack of real aggression in these situations will probably be reason enough to not offer you the job at all.

I think you should always try to make a selling point while asking a question, but in this case, it's virtually an imperative: *"I tried to make my cover letter and resume memorable. I'm glad you appreciated their creativity. Will that same 'out of the box' thinking be valued in this position?"*

INTERVIEW KILLERS

I'm going to assume that you have already been on enough interviews (or, if you're a recent graduate, read enough inter-viewing books) to know that there are rules to follow during interviews. So I'm not going to discuss most of them here.

But there is a list of "no-no's" that are so important, failing to avoid them can virtually doom *any* chance you have of secur-ing the job—before the interview even starts. Given their seri-ousness, I thought it prudent to remind you of them.

For many interviewers, your **showing up late** is immediate cause for canceling the interview. It doesn't matter that traffic backed up, your cat threw up a hairball, or you just got lost in the elevator.

Being on time is not racing down the final corridor with moments to spare. Some interviewers agree with New York Giants football coach Tom Coughlin—being late is not being fifteen minutes *early.*

Poor grooming is a basic turn-off. Wearing so much perfume or cologne that a gasping interviewer has to lunge for the window makes a poor first impression. So does wearing more makeup than a runway model, clanking along with a pocketful of change or an armload of bangles and bells, or trying out a blond-streaked Mohawk haircut.

Do I really have to tell you, ladies, that a dark suit, pearls, and pumps is **appropriate dress** for every interview? Given the tube tops, sneakers, short skirts, and patterned stockings I've seen waltz through my door (and all on one candidate!), maybe I do.

Men should wear a white or light blue shirt, conservative suit, silk tie and shined dress shoes.

No one should think of wearing ties that glow in the dark, T-shirts advertising anything (but especially not X-rated!), or any clothes deemed "relaxed and comfortable" (unless you are relaxed and comfortable in a double-breasted suit).

In case you haven't gotten the message (where have you been?), **smoking is no longer acceptable behavior** . . . anywhere, at any time. And don't kid yourselves—just because you don't light up during an interview doesn't mean that everyone in the room doesn't know you smoke.

Of course, if you decide to smoke during the interview itself (and some people have in my office), you can go down to that front door right away to finish up. Just don't plan on coming back upstairs.

Do not smoke even if the interviewer lights up and encourages you to do likewise.

There should be a new reality series featuring the **bizarre behavior** of some interviewees as they chew, burp, scratch, swear, cry, laugh, and scream their way into our hearts. Interviewees have shown up drunk or stoned, brought their mothers with them, fallen asleep, and even gone to the bathroom and never returned.

Keeping your cell phone on during the interview qualifies as inappropriate behavior. Actually receiving or making a call qualifies as bizarre.

Remember what the interviewer is undoubtedly thinking: If this is your *best* behavior, what (*gasp!*) do I have to look forward to?

If you **lie about anything,** especially where and when you worked, what you did, or where and when (or even if) you attended college, you will be caught. No matter how lowly the job, there are significant expenses involved with hiring someone to perform it. So companies will take the time to check out references. And the higher up the food chain, the more intensive their scrutiny.

Even if the lie is inconsequential, the very fact that you lied will, in virtually all instances, be immediate grounds for dismissal. Lacking a particular skill or experience may not automatically exclude you from getting the job. Lying about it will.

While honesty may be the best (and only) policy, it is **not necessary to share anything and everything** with your interviewer. He is not your priest, and you are not in a confessional. Anything you do in the privacy of your own home is not something you need to share.

So do be smart enough, when asked what interests you about the job, not to answer, *"Heck, I just need a job with benefits. I owe way too much on my Visa."*

Don't underestimate the effect of your body language on the interviewer. While many people don't mean what they say or say what they mean, their nonverbal actions reveal *exactly* what they're feeling. According to studies, *more than half* of what we are trying to communicate is being received nonverbally.

To many interviewers, your **failure to look them in the eye** indicates you have something to hide. So does being overly fidgety or nervous. Greet the interviewer with a firm handshake, face him or her, sit straight up and, of course, look 'em in the eye. *Breaking* eye contact occasionally is also a good idea. Staring at someone without pause for more than a few seconds will make them nervous.

Likewise, interviewers are looking for people who are **enthusiastic** about what they do, so sighing, looking out the window, or checking your watch during a question is not creating the right impression. If you don't seem interested in the job, why should they be interested in hiring you?

A candidate once said to me, barely five minutes into our interview, *"I've got three other offers right now. What can you do for me?"*

I showed him where the exit was.

Yes, you need to be confident, enthusiastic, and cheerful (and brave and clean and reverent . . .), but there can be, as this example clearly illustrates, too much of a good thing.

The interviewer asks what she thinks is a simple question and you act as if she has accused you of a crime. You start to sweat, hem and haw, and try to change the subject.

What are you hiding? That's what the interviewer will be wondering. And if you aren't actually hiding anything, why are you acting so defensively?

Interviewing over lunch is a situation fraught with potential dangers. Slurping spaghetti or wiping barbecue sauce off your tie is simply not attractive, even if you are. Ordering the most (or least) expensive item on the menu sends an unwelcome message. And what happens when the French dish you didn't understand but ordered anyway turns out to be sautéed brains?

If you can't avoid a lunch interview (and I would certainly try), use your common sense. Order something light and reasonably priced—you're not *really* there for the food, are you? Remember what Mom told you: Keep your elbows off the table, don't talk with your mouth full, and put your napkin on your lap. Don't drink alcohol (even wine), don't smoke (even if your host does), don't complain about the food (even if it was lousy), and don't forget that this is still an interview!

Although many interviewers will not consider inappropriate dress, poor grooming, or a bit too much candor an automatic reason for dismissal, an accumulation of two or more such actions may force even the most empathetic to question your suitability. (Some items, of course, such as dishonesty, may well lead to an immediate and heartfelt, *"Thank you . . . please don't stay in touch."*)

IS IT OKAY TO TAKE NOTES?

I suspect I could find equal numbers of recruiters, executives, and interviewers to come down on either side of this question. Of course, it's okay for the *interviewer* to take notes, which is why I believe it is okay for the interviewee too. Not just okay, but encouraged.

Why? There are a few good reasons:

First, you can't possibly remember everything, no matter how good your memory. And yet you certainly want to remember what *you* said, what *he* said, what seemed *right,* what felt *wrong,* titles, numbers . . . all the myriad things that went on during the interview. As long as you ask permission first, I believe taking notes is an absolute requirement.

Second, it is essential for your follow up. I encourage you to write brief individual notes to *every* person you meet on an interview, from the receptionist to the person who got your coffee, and even more targeted and longer letters to all the people with whom you actually interviewed. How can you be sure of the spelling of that many names, titles, and the like, without good notes? How can you make sure to answer (again) the objection you know may be the key thing obstructing your hiring? How can you schmooze the colleague who seemed a little cold to your candidacy, perhaps jealous because *he* wanted (or expected) your job?

Third, you may need to use your notes during the interview itself, jotting down a question you don't want to forget (while the interviewer drones on), a point you want to raise, or an example you want to emphasize. This will allow you to interject something at just the right time, which may be quite a while down the road, even at the very end of the interview.

I believe many if not most interviewers will interpret your note taking as a sign of professionalism and seriousness, as long as you don't lug in an iBook or Palm Pilot and keep your nose buried in it the entire time.

You should walk in with notes—the questions you intend to ask, detailed notes on financials, specific points you want to remember, and research data you want to incorporate in an answer or question. Getting the interviewer used to your "consulting my notes" makes it a lot easier to ask permission to *take* notes during the interview itself. But be careful. You don't want to appear to be constantly "referring to your notes" every time the interviewer asks a question: *"Where did you go to college, Jim?"* *"Uh, just a minute, let me consult my notes."*

Personally, I wouldn't want anything but an attractive notebook that is extracted from an equally professional-looking attaché case, along with a quality pen (not a disposable!). I find the use of a notebook computer much too distracting (as an interviewer), but it may be acceptable in high-tech industries where the interviewer could consider such technology a given (even a plus).

I'd never recommend a tape recorder, unless you plan to arrest the interviewer immediately after the interview. I see no positive value and a host of potentially negative reactions to it.

Whatever you use, remember the point of the interview is to listen, then talk. Write as little as you need to. And if you aren't very good at note taking and listening at the same time (or taking notes while retaining eye contact), practice. No one wants to talk to your forehead.

DON'T RUN AWAY . . . YET

We've all been there—an interview that is obviously not working. Maybe it's the interviewer, maybe it's you, maybe it's the weather, maybe it's a cruel joke by God. Whatever. The interview is not going well, and you are sorely tempted to get up, thank the interviewer, and run, not walk, to the safety of your bedroom.

Don't leave. Excuse yourself, perhaps for a bathroom break. (Hey, I know it's not usually done, but right now we're trying to salvage an interview that's going down in flames.) Compose yourself. Give yourself a pep talk. Then go back in there and sell yourself.

You may actually be completely unqualified for the job, which is why the interview is not going well. But that doesn't mean there aren't other jobs at that company or jobs at other companies the interviewer knows. Make the sale.

Questions to Ask Yourself

Who are you?

What are your strengths?

What is important to you?

What specific things do you require in the job you're seeking—adventure, glamour, a bigger office, more money?

Where do want to work?

What sized company do you want to work for?

How many people would you like working under you?

What are your long-term goals?

What are your short-term goals?

What have you already done to accomplish these short-term goals?

What do you still need to do?

Whew! And you were afraid the *interviewer* was going to ask tough questions!

There are a lot of questions to ask *yourself* long before you let your fingers wander through the want ads.

Answering these questions should enable you to define both short- and long-term goals—personal, professional, and financial—and could even help you develop a road map to reach those dreams. Additionally, they will help you better assess the fit between a company's culture, the job, the boss . . . and *you*. Unless you do this kind of analysis, on what basis will you be evaluating job offers? As the old saying goes, "if you don't know where you're going, any road will take you there."

So let's make a few lists to help you assess who you are, what's important to you, and what this analysis should tell you about the kind of company you want to work for. You'll quickly see that this is a far more detailed and completely different assessment than you were advised to do when collecting data for your resume.

QUESTIONS ABOUT YOU AS A PERSON

What are your key values?

What kinds of people do you enjoy spending time with?

Describe your personality.

What activities do you most like doing?

What activities do you least like doing?

Are you a risk-taker or risk averse?

What in your personal life causes you the most stress (relationships, money, time constraints, etc.)?

What in your personal life gives you the most pleasure?

If you had to spend 40 hours a week doing a single activity, what would it be?

What were your favorite subjects in school? Would they still be your favorites today?

What were your strongest subjects?

What games and sports do you enjoy? What does the way you play them say about you?

Are you overly competitive? Do you give up too easily?

Are you a good loser or a bad winner?

Do you rise to a challenge or back away?

What kinds of friends do you tend to have? Do you seek out people who are just like you or those who will laugh at all of your jokes?

What has caused you to break up friendships? What does this say about you?

If you were to ask a group of friends and acquaintances to describe you, what adjectives would *they* use? Why do you think they would describe you in those terms? Are there specific behaviors, skills, achievements, or failures that caused them to choose those adjectives? What are they?

QUESTIONS ABOUT YOU AS A PROFESSIONAL

What kinds of people do you like working with? What kinds do you dislike working with?

What are your goals and aspirations?

What would it take to transform yourself into someone who's passionate about every workday?

What *are* your passions?

How can you make yourself more marketable in today's competitive job market?

LIST YOUR CURRENT STRENGTHS, ABILITIES, AND VALUES

The following list of descriptive adjectives should help you further define who you really are, both professionally and personally. Circle those words or phrases that you believe describe you, and keep them in mind when assessing any job offer or any company and its attendant culture.

Active	Communicative
Active in sports	Computer literate
Active reader	Confident
Active volunteer	Courteous
Adaptable	Creative
Adventurous	Decisive
Ambitious	Dedicated
Artistic	Detail-oriented
Attractive	Directed
Brave/heroic	Dynamic
Calm	Economical

Efficient	Graceful
Empathetic	Handle stress well
Ethical	Hard-working
Excellent analytical skills	High energy
Excellent math skills	Highly educated (level?)
Experienced	Honest
Extrovert	Introverted
Flexible	Learn from mistakes
Fluent in other languages	Left-brained
Focused	Like people
Goal-oriented	Like to travel
Good delegating skills	Logical
Good leadership skills	Love animals
Good listening skills	Love children
Good mathematical skills	Loyal
Good negotiating skills	Make friends easily
Good presentation skills	Moral
Good public speaking skills	Musical
Good sense of humor	Neat
Good team-building skills	Obsessive
Good time management skills	Organized
Good under pressure	Passionate
Good written communicator	Passive

Patient	Risk averse
Perfectionist	Risk taker
Performer	Sales personality
Physically strong	Self-motivated
Precise	Sports fan
Professional	Strong-willed
Quick-thinking	Supportive of others
React well to authority	Tenacious
Religious	Welcome change
Responsible	Well-groomed
Right-brained	(Other) _____

These are all positive attributes, of one kind or another, to one company or another. After you've circled all of those you believe best describe you, ask your friends if they agree with your assessment.

You can use this list in a few important ways. First, it will help you better answer two key questions:

How do these positives match up with the qualities you believe are necessary for success in the job/career path you've chosen?

Do you have the qualities generally associated with the level of responsibility/job title you are seeking?

Let's say you are seeking a promotion to vice president at a major corporation, which would mean significant financial responsibility and hundreds of employees under your benevolent control. You will have a problem getting an interview, let alone the job, if you can't demonstrate managerial, team-building, motivational, and financial skills and experience (among others). So if you lack all or most of those characteristics, your current goal isn't realistic, and you must create a plan to attain the skills and experience you need to reach your professional goals.

Another important question is suggested by this list:

How many of these qualities/abilities do you *want* to use in your job?

Alternately, how many of the qualities you've deemed most important to your sense of self do you *need* to involve in your job? Only you can figure this out, but I suspect most people would be happy if their jobs utilized *more* of their abilities and interests rather than fewer. The happiest people I've ever met are those able to employ the qualities, skills, and talents they deem important at a company at which *those specific attributes* lead to success.

Another way to utilize this list is to identify qualities you lack but deem important to your next job or your future career. This will enable you to create a plan to develop, attain, or obtain what you want and need to succeed in your chosen path and reach your expressed goals.

WHAT KIND OF LIFE ARE YOU SEEKING?

How can you know what you want if you haven't taken the time to assess what's really important to you? Look at the list of values below (adapted from *Targeting the Job You Want,* one of an excellent series produced by The Five O'Clock Club, a top job-search group). Rate how important each is to you ("1" for least important, "4" for most):

Adventure	Helping society
Being considered an expert	Independence
Challenging tasks	Influencing people
Chance to advance	Intellectual stimulation
Chance to create	Leadership
Chance to grow	Meeting challenges
Chance to have an impact	Money
Chance to lead	Moral fulfillment
Chance to learn	Personal growth
Chance to participate	Power
Clear expectations	Prestige
Clear procedures	Public contact
Competition	Recognition from peers
Creativity	Recognition from society
Enjoyable colleagues	Recognition from superiors
Enjoyable surroundings	Slow pace
Enjoyable tasks	Stability (security)
Excitement	Structure
Fast pace	Time with family
Freedom from worry	Working alone
Glamour	Working for something you believe in
Having responsibility	
Helping people	Working on a team

Of those descriptions marked "4," identify the five *most* important to you right now. Then, of *those* five, admit which you would give up (if any) if you had to. Which would you *never* give up, no matter what?

Based on this exercise, you should be able to compose a brief paragraph describing the values of the company you'd (ideally) want to work for and the job you'd (ideally) love to have.

THE PRACTICAL ASPECTS OF YOUR JOB HUNT

In addition to assessing the kind of person you are, which will give you a better idea of the kind of people you want to work with and the environment in which you want to work, there are some more mundane questions you need to ask yourself:

Where (geographically) do I want to work?

Do I prefer a large city, small city, town, or somewhere as far away from civilization as possible?

Do I prefer a warm or cold climate?

Do I prefer a large or small company? (Define your terms—by sales, income, employees, etc.)

What kinds of products/services/accounts would I prefer to work with?

Do I mind traveling frequently? What percentage of my time is "reasonable"?

How much time am I willing to devote to a daily commute? At what point will its length impact my other priorities (family, hobbies, etc.)?

What salary would I like to receive?

What's the *lowest* salary I'll accept?

Are there any benefits (such as an expense account, medical and/or dental insurance, company car, etc.) I must or would like to have?

Am I planning to attend graduate school at some point in the future? If so, is it important that a tuition reimbursement plan be part of the company benefits package?

Is it important that the company have a formal employee-training program?

WHAT CAN YOU LEARN FROM PAST JOBS AND BOSSES?

For each job you've held in the past, describe those factors that made one enjoyable, satisfying, or rewarding and another boring, frustrating, or just plain hell. Be as specific as possible. Consider everything from the company's location, the size of its (or your) offices, perks (or lack thereof), your subordinates and supervisors, responsibilities (or lack thereof), promotional opportunities, and hours.

The more comprehensive you make this analysis, the more easily you will begin to identify behavioral patterns. This exercise may help you hone in on a particular requirement (a corner office), something to avoid at all costs (a boss who's passive-aggressive), or even some aspect of your own personality that you need to work on (lamenting a lack of promotional opportunities when you've never stayed at any job longer than six months!).

What can I learn from past bosses?

How well do I interact with authority figures— bosses, teachers, parents?

Even if every other aspect of a job is wonderful, you could be dying to move on just because you hate your boss. Hey, it happens. So before you extract yourself from the frying pan and deposit yourself directly into the fire, you might want to do the following exercise as well: Make a list of every boss you've ever had, using the broadest possible definition of "boss." Divide them into three lists: those with whom you *never* had a problem, those with whom you had *some* problems, and those with whom you *always* seemed to have problems.

After you've developed these three lists, try to identify the common factors that would explain the problems you had with the third group. Were they all old married white men who smoked cigars? Were they all fast-charging sales types? Were they all bosses for the same kinds of companies (large, small, whatever)?

You get the idea. The more you know about the kinds of bosses under whom you've thrived and those beneath whom you've withered, the better chance you have of finding the right fit the next time around.

I'll use myself (again) as an example: One of my early jobs in magazine publishing was as an advertising sales representative for a trade magazine. I was ambitious, passionate, and a very good salesperson. After teaching me about the basics of ad sales, my first boss pretty much kept out of the way and let me run. Boy, did I run! I set a single-year sales record that, I've been told, still stands.

Now, I didn't exactly do everything by the book. In fact, I threw the book away. I ignored *all* requests to do memos or reports or anything that would have taken time away from making sales (i.e., making more money). I did not communicate, I did not summarize, I did not report. I just sold. After a short time, my boss simply stopped asking for that stuff and decided to revel in the big jump his own income was taking due to my unbridled efforts.

I did so well I got promoted to a bigger magazine, becoming the youngest sales manager in that company's history. My old boss went to my new boss and sang my praises. But he also told her, in virtually these terms, to just *"let him the ___ alone. He's a maverick and won't follow any of your rules. He will make you a fortune, but he doesn't need to learn anything from you. Just let him sell and motivate his salespeople to sell."*

Well, my new boss wasn't nearly as flexible as my old boss had been (nor, obviously, as bright). Instead of adopting the recommended hands-off attitude, she wasted days of my time in a series of meetings explaining "how we do things at *this* magazine." It was a disaster from the get-go, and it wasn't long before it was made pretty clear (by the VP of Sales) that one of us was not going to be left standing.

A tremendous opportunity to move up to publisher of a major consumer travel publication materialized, as if on command. It represented a huge jump in responsibility and an equally huge jump in money. The only downside was that if I wanted the job, I would have to move to the Midwest, though I and my wife were confirmed New Yorkers. Plus, of course, she had a job she loved and informed me in no uncertain terms that she didn't intend to sacrifice her career for mine. (Good for her!) If my new boss had simply followed my first boss's advice, I probably would have turned the job down and continued on my well-planned rise at that trade publisher.

Well, she didn't. So I had little choice. Luckily, my wife's boss found a way for her to keep her job . . . and do it from the Midwest. So we moved. While the situation looked fantastic, it turned out to be a company in well-hidden trouble with *two* control-freak bosses (a husband and wife, no less) that I reported to. Within ten months, I was looking for a job again . . . and making the move back to the New York area . . . where no one particularly wanted to give me a job approaching the money or responsibility I had just had!

The result was a company called Career Press, which I founded not long thereafter, using my severance check from the Midwest. More than two decades later, it is a well-known publisher of 72 nonfiction books a year.

Now, I am not at all unhappy that things worked out the way they did. I became my own boss, and I have absolutely never regretted the unexpected path my career took. But it wasn't exactly a free choice, was it? It started with a *promotion,* of all things. Did I ask *anything* about that first new boss? How compatible we were? Her style of management? Did I talk to anyone else that had worked for her? Did I talk to my predecessor in that position?

NO.

Did I ask about the salary and bonuses and special deals? Oh, you betcha I did.

It gets worse. Because I was in an untenable situation, the Midwest job looked like a godsend. Well, did I ask *anything* about my two new bosses before starting to pack? How compatible we were? Their (absolutely contradictory) styles of management? Did I talk to anyone else who had worked for them? Did I talk to my predecessor in that position?

You know the answers, right?

I do not handle authority well, something I guess I knew in my heart. But I never took the time to analyze myself enough to discover how essential a part of my nature it really was. Even after it caused one meltdown, I walked right into a second.

A single aspect of *your* personality can have a similar affect on your relationship with a boss or company. Take the time to know yourself well enough to at least anticipate a problem!

DON'T WEAR SANDALS AT A WHITE-SHOE COMPANY

Birds of a feather *do* flock together. And different companies tend to attract particular "species" of employees. A company's physical environment, management attitude and policies, and the personality of the "birds" that predominate, comprise its corporate culture. Is it a loose atmosphere, with jean-clad creative types running amok? Or a buttoned-down, blue-suited autocracy, with a long list of rules to follow during timed coffee breaks?

Some companies are dominated by a single personality—a still-active founder or an executive who has exerted a strong, long-lasting influence on policies and style. Think Jack Welch at GE, Bill Gates at Microsoft, or Larry Ellison at Oracle. While there are exceptions, such companies tend to be closely held fiefdoms whose every level reflects the "cult of personality." If that personality is a despot, benign or otherwise, even a decentralized management structure won't create a company everyone wants to work for. (Gates, for one, is reportedly a very difficult boss.)

Family-owned companies often pose similar problems. Your chances to make decisions and take responsibility may be tied to your last name. Barely competent family members may wind up with cushy, highly paid jobs, while you and other "outsiders" do all the work. While many such firms are privately held, even publicly traded companies in which family members hold a significant block of stock (like Ford or Dupont) still answer primarily to the family.

Many larger, more decentralized companies will spread decision-making power and opportunities for advancement somewhat more evenly. However, such companies often encourage competition among workers, rather than focusing their collective energies on competing organizations, products, or services.

If managers regularly spend half their time politicking or writing self-serving memos to the boss, it's a survival-of-the-fittest (or survival-of-the-best-memo-writer) atmosphere. People attuned to corporate infighting might relish such a company; those who just want to do their jobs and be rewarded for the work they do will find it an unfriendly place to work.

Some companies are bursting with energy. Their offices seem to reverberate with a steady hum of activity. Such a high-key environment is right for aggressive go-getters who are unafraid of such a fast pace and more than ready, even eager, to jump into the fray. Other workplaces are calmer, quiet, almost studious in nature. Such low-key firms are probably better choices for more laid-back personalities.

While a high-energy or low-key atmosphere says little about a particular company's chances for success, it may have a lot to do with your own on-the-job performance, success, and happiness. Matching dissimilar corporate and individual personalities usually results in a new job search.

If you run across a company that seems to give off no signals at all, beware! This is usually the directionless organization, one that lacks both an agenda and dynamic leadership. Without such leadership, you can be certain that this organization will founder, usually when things start going wrong and the timely implementation of company-wide decisions is required.

Clearly, the more you know about the companies you're considering, the better off you'll be. For those of you—and that should be *all* of you—who want to research a specific company and/or job description, Chapter 3 will give you the necessary hints and resources.

Once you've analyzed yourself and investigated a targeted company's culture, a simple but extremely important question should come to mind:

How does your self-description match that of the culture at the company you're thinking of joining?

If you are laid back and not particularly driven to overachieve, a company that describes itself as "hard-charging" may not be for you, even if you can actually convince them to hire you.

The Gallup Organization is a unique example of corporate culture. When my good friend Tony Rutigliano was recruited by them, their offer was so enticing that it seemed like a "no-brainer" . . . until Tony asked about exactly what he'd be doing, his job title, and to whom he'd be reporting.

"*Well,*" the recruiter confided, "*we work a little differently here. We expect that you'll wander around for a while, maybe a few months, and then you'll tell us what you really want to do. We don't really have formal job descriptions. And you can use any reasonable title.*"

Needless to say, Tony, a veteran of a number of traditional magazine publishing companies, was a bit taken aback. Wander around? Create his own job description? Choose his own title?

Since Tony was a bit of an entrepreneur at heart and a confident bloke to boot, he decided to give it a try. Luckily for him, Gallup's corporate culture, as unusual as it was, turned out to be a great fit for him.

Would it have been an equally rewarding and ultimately successful move for you? Not if you were someone who expected or required a rigid organizational chart. Anyone too uncomfortable to just "wander about" would probably have run for the hills after a couple of days (presuming they were crazy enough to take the job in the first place).

There may be nothing inherently wrong with an organization you're considering—it just might be a horrible fit *for you,* one that could throw you completely off the career track you have outlined. Maybe you will survive, maybe you will thrive, maybe you will find yourself looking for another job in six months. Or maybe it will cause you to positively change your goals. In any event, you must know what you're getting into and do everything you can to prepare for that environment.

THE IMPORTANCE OF GOALS

I've mentioned the importance of goals already. Now it's time to emphasize them. Short- and long-term goal setting must become a habit. Once a year, reevaluate not just the progress you're making toward your long-term goals, but whether they need to be tweaked, heavily modified, or even changed completely. Life is not static. Neither are your goals; they will (and should) change with circumstance, age, position, and the like.

Remember that setting goals will not only help you define where you want to go, but what you need to know and do to get there. If you have decided that you eventually want to be Chief Financial Officer of a large corporation, you may well need an MBA or similar graduate degree. When do you plan to get it? Would you go to graduate school full- or part-time? If the latter, will the company allow a modified work schedule so you can go to school while you work? Does the company offer a tuition reimbursement plan? Is there already a program in place to which you can apply? Your goals, and your estimation of what you need to do and be to reach them, will greatly influence the questions you ask.

It's equally important to make your goals realistic. There is nothing wrong with reaching for the stars, providing you have the right-sized step stool. If you aren't a high school graduate, you *can* aspire to becoming chairman of IBM, but your short-term goals better include some serious additional education! If you want to be a prize-winning author, passing a creative writing class might be a nice first step. Goals are realistic if there is a clear-cut path that you can follow to reach them. It may be a hard and long road, but if you truly believe you can actually reach its end with sufficient effort, then the goal is realistic.

Even if a goal is completely *un*realistic, I would not necessarily counsel you to drop it. First of all, who's to say it really *is* unrealistic? You may have little or no natural writing ability and couldn't draw a straight line if your life depended on it. Would I be willing to bet you probably *won't* become the creative director of one of the world's top three advertising agencies? Well, I'm a betting man, so I probably *would* take that bet. But the human spirit is an amazing thing. Who says with the right education, jobs, and practice that your goal, though "unrealistic," couldn't be realized? And even if it weren't, the additional education and dedication certainly wouldn't hurt your career prospects!

What if the goal is realistic, but you are simply unwilling or unable to do what's necessary to reach it? Change it—why kid yourself? While luck plays a factor in many careers, it is certainly not the only factor; the one common denominator of virtually any success story is hard work. If you aren't willing to work hard, almost *any* goal may be unrealistic.

Your immediate and future personal/financial goals will, of course, have a great effect on your decision making and on the questions you ask (and answers you absolutely need to know). If you're unmarried and childless and someone actually offers to pay you to wander the globe, you may be more than all right with the arrangement. But what if you anticipate getting married or having kids in a year or two? What if you know you have to prepare to take care of an older relative? Your financial needs may dramatically change. The kind of hours, travel, and work load that you're willing to take on now may need to be radically overhauled. You may not mind relocating once a year *now* but resist relocating at all after you've "settled down." If you have chosen a job/career/industry/company in which declining to relocate may mean the *end* of your job/career, your future plans must be part of your current equation.

SHOW ME THE MONEY!

What is your current standard of living, and are you happy with it?

Can you comfortably afford your current lifestyle, or are you living beyond your means with nothing in the bank and a fistful of maxed-out credit cards?

What standard of living do you aspire to in 2 years? 5 years? 10?

What salary (or package) is required to meet these targets?

Besides salary, what benefits or package components do you consider essential? Nice? Unnecessary?

Answering these questions is obviously important. You have to realistically define your financial wants and needs. How can you know how much you need if you can't figure out how to live on what you've got right now? Develop a budget. Develop a financial plan.

As you analyze the cost of some of your long-range planning, you're going to shock yourself. Especially if you are a recent college graduate, laying out what "life" costs could be daunting. But don't forget to look at the other side of the coin—what you're going to earn. Even if your starting salary were $25,000 and you never got a better job or a raise (and leaving out the costs of inflation, which is just a pain in the butt anyway), if you work for 40 years, you'll earn $1 million. Earn, on average, $50,000 a year, and you'll wind up making $2 million. And if you quickly ascend to that $100,000 a year level? That's right—$4 million or more 40 years from now.

If you are (hopefully) given the choice between two or more jobs, you need some basis on which to decide between them. If one job pays substantially less than the other but is much closer to your ideal career path, has more promise, or has some other greatly appealing quality, you really need to know whether you can afford to take it . . . because you very much might *want* to take it, despite the lower pay.

You need to look farther into the future than tomorrow. Companies still do survive and thrive, and a company you're considering (especially if it is a non-hi-tech behemoth that's been a Fortune 500 company for decades) may very well be around when your grandkids are reading this book. What does this mean in terms of your job hunt? Your financial prospects at that firm 2, 5, or even 10 years in the future may be very relevant indeed. Taking a position that pays less than you would like at a company where you believe (based on your research, conversations, maybe even promises from the interviewer) your financial goals could well be reached or even exceeded farther down the line, may be a smart move. And the bigger the company, the more likely there will be significant opportunities to change jobs, even areas (hence, careers), without leaving the company.

What if you are offered more, perhaps *substantially* more, rather than less? Simple question: What will you earn if you're fired or quit after a month, or three, or six? Isn't that a reality you need to at least consider?

If you choose a job purely because it pays substantially more, and the job (or the company!) disappears after a month, or two, or three, what have you actually made? A heck of a lot less than you thought you were getting! Suddenly a $12,000 annual difference becomes a difference of $3,000, $2,000, or even $1,000. Not to mention that you are now out of a job. How much are you losing while you find another job? Yep. More than the $12,000 on which your supposedly well-thought-out decision was based.

There's more to life than money, and money is only one aspect to consider about a job offer. Make sure you know enough about who you are, where you want to go, what you need, and what you want so you're ready to make an *informed* decision, not just a comparison of dollars and cents.

This is not your grandfather's job market (or, for that matter, your mother's). There is no security. Do you remember (or have you heard about) those days when you took a job and could count on reasonable raises for 40 years or so until you retired with your gold watch? Those days are long gone, so making a decision to take a job that does not really fulfill your long-term goals (maybe not even many of your short-term goals) just because it pays more money (even a lot more money!) is not necessarily smart.

Interestingly, keeping money in this kind of perspective meshes nicely with the Five O'clock Club's notion of creating a "40-year vision" of your career. If you read any of the books by its founder, Kate Wendleton, you will see how often her members choose between three, five, or more offers and *wind up taking the one that pays the least in the short run.* This is not because each of them has decided that money is not as important as some of the other factors we've been discussing. In many cases, it's because they had a clear vision of the financial *potential* of each offer and made a more long-term decision.

Besides, I doubt there are many people who have fervently proclaimed on their deathbeds, *"I wish I had just worked harder"* or *"I just wish I had made another sale."* Always give personal goals the same weight as career/professional goals unless you have consciously decided to do otherwise. Most of us don't consciously decide anything of the sort; we just let the professional goals overwhelm the personal. We "become our jobs"—, which is not inherently a bad thing, but not a good one if it throws the rest of our lives completely out of balance.

Be careful how many of your decisions in life, including, of course, where you work, are based solely on money. The older I get, the more I see how many of the decisions I've had to make have been based far too much on money (either wanting or not having) and not nearly enough on conscious lifestyle choices. I feel sometimes, and I suspect many of you do, too, that money makes a mockery of the term "choices"—what do you mean, choices? A man's gotta do what a man can afford (or not).

Not to get into a Dennis Miller rant here, but if money isn't the root of all evil, it can certainly be considered the root of one heck of a lot of dissatisfaction. There are, at the risk of sounding simplistic, a lot of people without what many of us would consider "a lot of money" (define with your own number of zeros) who are quite content in their lives, thank you very much. And, of course, there are a plethora of "poor little rich kids" who seem to have received nothing but grief with their inherited zillions. So keep money in its place. It's important, even essential, but it ain't all there is.

ARE YOU MOVING TOO FAST?

Don't be too ready to give up what you already have (your current job) just because you believe the grass just has to be greener "over there." Ask yourself some smart questions first:

> **Can you achieve your ultimate career path in your current company?**
>
> **How does your current job differ from your ideal job?**
>
> **What specific skills and experience do you need to transform one into the other?**
>
> **How can you transfer skills you already have to a completely different career?**
>
> **How would you describe your absolute dream job? Where would you be? What would you be doing? Who would you be working with/for? What would you be earning?**
>
> **What additional education or training would you need to achieve this dream job? If you obtained the education or training but *didn't* attain the dream job, how do you think your current job or career path would be affected?**

You may be putting the cart before the horse if you're already gung-ho on interviewing at other companies but haven't asked yourself these important questions. You already have (one hopes) a good reputation at your current job. A good history. Friends. Experience. Respect. If all of that is true, you should want to move on only if your answers to the above questions are negative.

If there is *any* way to stay at your current job and/or at your current company if the answers are *positive*, think long and hard about why you would want to make a change. My advice would be to evaluate what you would need to do to create your ideal job *at your current company,* even if you hate your current job, current boss, or current situation. Analyze first what it would take to make you happy. And if you can fathom *any* way to do it without going through the job-search process, do so. It's a jungle out there, and better the frying pan you're already in than throwing yourself upon someone else's pyre.

Of course, this is a moot point if, having done the analysis, you conclude there is simply no viable way to get even remotely close to your ideal job at a compensation level that you need. Or if the very nature of the company (10 employees, a field you want out of completely, etc.) makes it moot.

But don't be afraid to ask the questions raised at the beginning of this section and, perhaps, two more:

> **Are there any training programs available that may make the kind of move you want possible?**

> **Presuming there *is* "room at the top," what specifically do you think you would have to do to earn the job title/salary/responsibilities/etc. you want? *Can* you do it? Within a timeframe you deem reasonable?**

By taking a more patient approach, you may give yourself the best of both possible worlds—working toward your goals at your *present* company while still testing the waters at others.

By the time you finish the exercises in this chapter, you should be ready to sit down and describe not just the companies you'd like to work for, but your duties and responsibilities, your new boss's personality, the people you will be working with, and where you'd like to be 2, 5, 10 . . . yes, even 40 years down the road. If you have honestly and completely answered the questions you asked of yourself, I think you will be able to do so.

Questions to Ask During Your Research

R esearch is an essential first step in any job search. If you know nothing about the firm, department, job, or boss, you have no real clue of how to position your answers to any of the interviewer's questions (or target your own questions). That's why you can't just go in with a bunch of basic questions that you could have easily answered yourself after a few hours at the library or online.

You have many skills and qualifications and talents, some or all of which may be pertinent, one of which may be key. How do you know? You won't.

So the research is not just to give you a set of questions to ask. It's to help you customize those questions and target your answers to the interviewer's questions.

Here's a complete checklist of the facts you should know about each company at which you schedule an interview:

The basics

1. Directions to the office you're visiting.

2. Headquarters location (if different).

3. Some idea of domestic and international branches.

4. Relative size (compared to other companies in the field).

5. Annual billings, sales, and/or income (last two years).

6. Subsidiary companies; specialized divisions.

7. Departments (overall structure).

8. Major accounts, products, or services.

9. Major competitors.

The not-so-basics

1. History of the firm (specialties, honors, awards, famous names).

2. Names, titles, and backgrounds of top management.

3. Existence (and type) of training program.

4. Relocation policy.

5. Relative salaries (compared to other companies in the field or by size).

6. Recent developments concerning the company and its products or services.

7. Everything you can learn about the career, likes, and dislikes of the person(s) interviewing you.

WHERE TO START LOOKING

For a very broad overview of any industry, consult the U.S. Bureau of Labor Statistics (http://stats.bls.gov), which uses business and economic trends and changing demographics to chart expected growth in employment for occupations in every industry over a 10-year period. The most current edition of the *Occupational Outlook Handbook* (2006–07 edition) is available here, as are online quarterly updates, a wealth of industry and economic information, and the most current (2004–05) edition of *The Career Guide to Industries,* the companion to the *OOH.* The *2004–05 Occupational Outlook Handbook, Official Government Job and Career Guide, plus Career Guide to Industries and a Huge Collection of Bureau of Labor Statistics (BLS) Documents,* a CD-ROM with over 26,000 pages of data, is also available.

In addition, here's a core list of research sources, many of which should be available in your local library:

- **THE ENCYCLOPEDIA OF BUSINESS INFORMATION SOURCES** (2005, 20th edition) lists some 25,000 sources on more than a thousand specific subjects, including directories, associations, and more. The annual *Directories in Print* (26th edition now available) organizes companies by industry. *Business Rankings* includes details on the nation's top 7,500 firms. (All from Thomson Gale.)

- **DIRECTORY OF CORPORATE AFFILIATIONS** (Lexis Nexis) better be available in your library—it weights 35 lbs. and costs $1,700!

- Dun and Bradstreet's family of corporate reference resources: the *Million Dollar Directory* (160,000 companies with a net worth of more than $500,000); *Top 50,000 Companies* (those with a minimum net worth of just under $2 million); and *Reference Book of Corporate Managements,* which provides detailed biographical data on the principal officers and directors of some 12,000 corporations. (Who says you can't find out about the quirks and hobbies of your interviewer?)

- **STANDARD AND POORS' REGISTER OF CORPORATIONS, DIRECTORS, AND EXECUTIVES** includes corporate listings for more than 45,000 firms as well as 72,000 biographical listings.

- **THOMAS REGISTER OF AMERICAN MANUFACTURERS** is an annual profile of more than 150,000 manufacturers and features information on primary products and services plus more than 100,000 trade and brand names.

- **WARD'S BUSINESS DIRECTORY OF U.S. AND PRIVATE COMPANIES** includes listings of nearly 100,000 companies, the majority of them privately held, and details that are usually the most difficult to acquire about such firms, such as number of employees, annual sales, and the like. The 48th edition (2005) is currently available; the 49th edition will be published in August 2006.

- **THE STANDARD DIRECTORY OF ADVERTISERS** (also known as the Advertiser Red Book, because of its bright red cover) lists more than 17,000 companies that commit some portion of their budgets to advertising and promotion. It is available in two editions—classified and geographical. Major product lines and the agencies to whom they are assigned are listed, as well as the names and job functions of key marketing personnel at the listed companies and their agencies.

- **THE FORTUNE 500** is an annual compilation by *Fortune* magazine of the top U.S. businesses, ranked by sales. It will become particularly important later in your search, when you're targeting specific companies. At that time, it will enable you to analyze not only where a particular company ranks in the overall U.S. economy but also whether it is falling or on the rise and how it measures up against other companies in its field.

Two other potential sources of leads include *The Oxbridge Directory of Newsletters,* a listing of thousands of newsletters in a range of industries, and *Trade Shows Worldwide: An International Directory of Events, Facilities and Suppliers* (Thomson Gale), which lists more than 2,000 trade shows and conventions. Why not consider attending some to learn more about the companies and products out there?

Become acquainted with a key reference resource—the various volumes of the Standard Rate and Data Service (SRDS), all of which are available in most libraries. The volume in which you're interested is Business Publications. In it you'll find a list, by industry, of the thousands of business (or trade) magazines currently being published.

These publications are prime sources of information, especially if you are relatively new to the job market. Start reading them regularly (many are collected in metropolitan public libraries). Write for recent issues of the leading publications in the fields you've targeted. If you make reading a weekly practice, you will accomplish a number of important goals. You'll begin to absorb information about:

- The industry as a whole.

- Major companies in the field.

- Trends, new products, and the general outlook for specific product categories.

- Major players in the industry, both companies and individuals.

- Industry/professional jargon or buzzwords.

In addition, published interviews with leading practitioners in the field will give you insight as to how they approach their specific jobs.

Finally, there are the major newspapers and magazines you should turn to now and then to complete your research: *The Wall Street Journal, Barron's, Business Week, Fortune, Forbes, Industry Week, Nation's Business, National Business Employment Weekly,* and *Inc.,* as well as the pertinent trade magazines in your field.

FINDING INFORMATION ON SMALLER COMPANIES

A majority of new jobs are created by small companies, but you may not learn much about them from most of the standard reference resources listed above. If your initial research proves fruitless or only marginally productive, try the following outside sources of information:

- **THE CHAMBER OF COMMERCE** in the community that's home to the company or division can help you assess how the company has been performing: Has it been growing or shrinking? How many people does it employ? How many did it employ in the community two years ago? Do people consider it a good place to work?

- **BUSINESS/INDUSTRY ASSOCIATIONS:** Many trade associations are excellent resources for industry data and statistics as well as general employment trends and specific opportunities. Three helpful resources are the *Encyclopedia of Associations* and *Business Organizations, Agencies and Publications Directory* (both from Thomson Gale) and

National Trade and Professional Associations of the United States (Columbia Books, Inc.).

● **EXECUTIVE, PROFESSIONAL, AND TECHNICAL PLACE-MENT AGENCIES:** If you are getting the job interview through an agency, see how much you can learn about the prospective employer from them (and see Chapter 4).

● **BUSINESS EDITORS:** Turn the tables on the news media—ask *them* the questions! A community newspaper's business reporter or editor will usually be the person most knowledgeable about local companies. They'll know about developments at particular companies, how employees like working for them, and their reputation in the community.

● **TRADE MAGAZINES:** Every industry has at least one trade magazine covering its developments. Call a junior (assistant or associate) editor. Ask if the publication has covered the company and, if so, how you can obtain copies of pertinent article(s).

● **SCHOOL ALUMNI:** A college placement office, your fraternity/sorority, or alumni association might be able to tell you about someone working at the company. Alumni are usually happy to help someone from their alma mater.

● **STOCKBROKERS/ANALYSTS:** If the company is public, it will have an investor relations representative who can tell you which brokers and analysts "follow the stock." This means that a representative of the brokerage firm has visited with the company, written a detailed report for investors, and analyzed its industry, balance sheet, and management. Call the broker and ask for a copy of the report. It will be objective, revealing, and give you terrific material with which to impress the interviewer.

● **ONLINE:** Start with the *Web Site Source Book 2005: A Guide to Major U.S. Businesses, Organizations, Agencies, Institutions and other Information Sources on the World Wide Web.* There are also a multitude of blogs, bulletin boards, databases, and discussion groups through which you can track down obscure information to impress a prospective employer in an interview. Your first step, of course, should be to check out the company's Web site.

Before you check out individual Web sites, consider using a meta engine, such as profusion, dogpile, or webcrawler, to "search the search engines." Then consider looking at some of the Web sites I've listed below. Most are for research; some are just for advice. Only one (the first) is hosted by a resume-writing service (and that's because of the excellent links the site offers):

www.1stresumes.com

www.6figurejobs.com

www.Acinet.org (America's Career Infonet, sponsored by the U.S. Dept. of Labor)

www.Ajb.dni.us (America's job bank)

www.Alumni-network.com (hi-tech jobs)

www.Bestjobsusa.com

www.Bilingual-jobs.com

www.Bizjournals.com (local business news from cities throughout the U.S.)

www.Businessweek.com

www.Businesswire.com

www.Career.com

www.Careerbuilder.com

www.Careerbuzz.com (hip and happening, but for young people only)

www.Careerjournal.com (a Wall Street Journal company)

www.Careermag.com

www.Careers.org (with 4,000 links to other sites)

www.Careershop.com

www.Ceoexpress.com

www.Collegegrad.com

www.Computerjobs.com

www.Corporateinformation.com

www.Cyberkingemployment.com (56 languages, 130 countries)

www.Dice.com (primarily technical careers)

www.Dnb.com (information on 10,000,000 U.S. companies from Dun and Bradstreet)

www.Employment911.com

www.Eresumes.com

www.Fiveoclockclub.com (one of the best job hunt sites)

www.Forbes.com

www.Guidestar.org (for nonprofits)

www.Hirediversity.com (if you're disabled)

www.Homefair.com (to compare cost of living by city and state)

www.Hoovers.com

www.Idexec.com (online access to 2 million decision makers at 900,000 companies worldwide)

www.Jobbankusa.com

www.Joblynx.com

www.Jobstar.org

www.Jobweb.com (college students)

www.Latpro.com (if you're fluent in Spanish or Portuguese)

www.Monster.com

www.Monstertrak.com (primarily for college students)

www.Nationjob.com

www.Nettemps.com (temp jobs)

www.Newslink.org (a worldwide directories of newspapers and magazines)

www.Prnewswire.com (news on companies and individuals)

www.Recruitersonline.com (more than 2,000 registered recruiters)

www.Reuters.com

www.Truecareers.com

www.Wageweb.com (salary info)

www.Wetfeet.com (though most of their insider guides are overpriced)

www.Worktree.com

www.Wsj.com (Wall Street Journal)

VAULT.COM

This site deserves special mention. Go to their message boards (the Electronic Water Cooler), which are organized by industry, company(!), university, law school, business school, even career topic. The day I last checked, there were 1,654,610 messages listed (some quite old, but the number is nevertheless impressive). Talk about getting the inside scoop! What a potential treasure trove of information!

ASK THE COMPANY ITSELF

Once you've culled the *outside*—and probably more objective— sources of information, take a look at what the company tells the public about itself. Check out the company's Web site and/or call the company's Investor Relations or Human Resources department to obtain the following:

- **ANNUAL REPORTS.** Mark Twain said that there are three kinds of lies—"lies, damned lies, and statistics"—and you'll find all of them in most annual reports. Read between the lines to learn as much as you can about the company.

  You will be able to tell how the company's sales and profits have been increasing or decreasing over the past few years, what its plans are for the years ahead, and the health of the industry in which it operates.

In addition, an annual report should indicate how the company feels about its employees. Note whether the report features accomplishments of particular employees. Does it have photos of people at work? Or does it focus strictly on "the numbers" and highlight the self-aggrandizing musings of the chairman?

- **EMPLOYEE HANDBOOKS.** Be gutsy. Ask the company to send you a copy of this valuable document. At the very least, the handbook will tell you about benefits, vacation time, salary-review policies, and other information you might not want to ask about in an initial interview. It also should give you valuable insights into the company's attitude toward its employees. Is in-house training provided? Is the company picnic a much-anticipated annual event?

- **SALES/MARKETING BROCHURES.** Knowing about a company's products will help you determine whether you'd like to work for the organization and will give you material upon which to base your questions.

- **COMPANY NEWSLETTERS.** There may be far more details about the company picnic than you would like, but there also might be some personal information about your interviewer, your future coworkers, or your future boss. You'll also get a better feel for how the company communicates with "the troops," how they view their future, new product launches, recent awards, and so on.

Although nobody likes doing it, homework does have its payoffs, especially during a job hunt. From the research you doggedly pursued on prospective employers, you should have learned several important things about each of the companies you targeted:

- What it's looking for in its employees.

- Its key products and markets.

- Whether it's hired employees from your school and how they've fared.

- Who the hiring manager is and what type of people he or she usually hires.

- Why you might enjoy working for that company.

All of this information will prove invaluable to you, not only during the interview, but in helping you get the interview in the first place.

Research from books, the Net, phone calls, interviews, and the like is all necessary, but don't disbelieve what your eyes and ears tell you if you visit the company. When you're waiting in the reception area, look around and listen up. What do the people seem like? Is it a loose atmosphere? Fast? Slow? Is there a lot of joking around? Does everyone who passes by look like a much-loved pet just died? Are they talking to each other, joking around, having fun? Or does it seem like a row of Dilberts in cubbyholes?

Plan to get to every interview early so you can play a little detective. Talk to everyone you meet: What do you do? How long have you worked here? Do you like it?

Questions to ask "Preinterviewers"

The questions in this chapter are those to *ask of anyone who lacks the final authority to hire you*. If you're relatively young and inexperienced, you may do a series of *informational interviews* to learn about an industry, company, or job you think you'd like. Depending on your level of experience, you may utilize an employment agency, recruiting firm, or headhunter. And even if you know you should do everything to avoid them, you may find yourself interviewing, on the phone or in person, with a Human Resources staffer.

None of these people can offer you a job. But all of them can offer you something almost as valuable: the information about the company, position, and hiring manager you *do* need to land that job.

This chapter will show you how to utilize each of these "preinterviewers" and the questions to ask them.

INFORMATION PLEASE

An **informational interview** should be utilized by someone either new to the job market (i.e., a recent high school or college graduate) or an experienced worker seeking a career change.

There is a huge difference between a job interview and an informational interview. In an informational interview, your goal is to learn as much as possible about the industry, company, and job you've targeted (although such an interview may come very early in the job-search process, long before you've begun to pursue specific companies or even a specific industry). If you are actively seeking a job at a specific company, such an interview is rarely one you would schedule at that company; rather, you should seek out a similar company in the same industry.

If you are more concerned with learning about a particular job description, not as picky about the industry, and not ready to hone in on specific companies, then you could seek an informational interview with someone in the same position at virtually *any* company in *any* industry.

A meeting with someone already doing what you soon *hope* to be doing is by far the best way to find out what you need to know *before* a formal job interview. You'll find that most people are happy to talk about their jobs. I know I often sit down with "friends of friends" and share what I've learned about book publishing. Because there is no immediate pressure on me to evaluate that "friend" as a candidate, I can be more informal, forthcoming, and relaxed.

You may learn of a specific job opening during an informational interview. If so, you are in an enviable position to unearth many important details about it. You may learn the identity of the actual interviewer (or, more important, the decision maker) and, if you're lucky, something about her experience, values, and personality. With your contact's permission, you may even be able to use his name as a referral.

As you prepare to conduct informational interviews, there are, ideally, six individual goals you hope to fulfill during each:

1. To unearth current information about the industry, company, and pertinent job functions. Remember: Gaining knowledge and understanding of broad industry trends, the financial health of the industry and its key players, hiring opportunities, and the competitive picture are key components in your search for the right job.

2. To investigate each company's hiring policies: Who makes the decisions? Who are the key players? Is there a hiring season?

3. To sell yourself and leave a calling card, your resume.

4. To seek out advice to help you refine your job search.

5. To obtain referrals to expand your network of contacts.

6. To develop a list of follow-up activities that will heighten your visibility among your key contacts.

Of course, the line between the people who can give you information about a certain field you've targeted and potential employers in that field can sometimes blur. Don't be concerned—you'll soon learn when (and how) to shift the focus from interview*er* to interview*ee*.

To simplify this process, follow a single rule: Show interest in the industry or job area under discussion, but never aggressively seek out information about particular openings; wait until the interviewer raises the possibility of your working there. You may be surprised at how often the person you're interviewing turns to you and asks, *"Would you be interested in _____ [a current job opening]?"* If you *would* be interested in the position under discussion, by all means make your feelings known.

SMART QUESTIONS DURING AN INFORMATIONAL INTERVIEW

In addition to any questions your research failed to answer (which, of course, you should now ask), here are some other smart questions to ask during any informational interview:

What are your duties and responsibilities?

How do you spend your day?

How did you get started at this company (or in your profession)?

What do you like most about your job? What do you like least?

What kind of person do you think is right for this kind of work?

What skills are in short supply here? (Careful: This is bordering on the aggressive!)

How can I learn more about this field? Are there specific trade journals I should be reading or associations I can join?

How can I meet others in this field?

What is the best way to get started (in this field or at this company)? This is a question for recent graduates to ask.

I'm trying to get in to see people at some other organizations. Do you know anyone at these companies? May I use your name?

Given my credentials, where would you see me fitting in at a company like yours?

This is probably as close to a "closing" question as you want in an informational interview. At worst, you'll get some valuable advice. At best, you may just get yourself a real interview.

Can you direct me to others in your department/ organization/division/company with whom you think it would be appropriate for me to talk or meet?

Now, it's possible that the interviewer will direct you to another person or two for the express purpose of educating you. After all, that *is* what you said you were there for. But there is another positive possibility: You may have impressed him. In fact, despite your assertion that you're "just seeking information," he may be thinking, *"Hmmm, this guy is good. He may be right for that opening in Josh's department."* In which case you have just transformed an informational interview into a job interview . . . with this single question. That's why I like it!

INTERVIEWING WITH RECRUITERS, HEADHUNTERS, EMPLOYMENT AGENCIES

Of the many outside counselors who can help with your job search or arm you with job leads, employment agencies are on the bottom rung of the ladder. Dozens of them may get the same job openings from the same companies at the same time. Candidates are a bit like fast-food customers: first come, first served.

Recruiters are a decided step up, although not all of them work on an exclusive basis. So, again, there may be more than one or two of them seeking similar candidates for the same openings.

Headhunters are the top of the ladder, generally working in specific fields (mining, engineering, media, etc.) for companies seeking professional, even executive, employees at decidedly higher pay scales.

The higher up the food chain you go, the more the counselor is likely to know about the company, the job, and the interviewer.

Once an agency, recruiter, or headhunter believes you to be a qualified and serious candidate for a position (i.e., you're going after a job for which you're qualified and, in her opinion, have a reasonable chance of getting hired), you can use them as great initial sources of information. In fact, questions that would be inappropriate or uncomfortable to ask on a "real" interview may be fine to ask a recruiter or headhunter.

Just remember that these counselors are working for the company—that's who's paying their fees and probably giving them dozens of medium- to high-level jobs to fill every year. So, ultimately, that's where their loyalties lie. Nevertheless, if they can supply a key client with its newest superstar—you— their stock will rise accordingly. (We won't mention what happens if you embarrass them on the job or, worse, on the interview, will we?)

Here are some key questions to ask agencies and recruiters:

What is the company?

How long have you been working with this company?

The longer they've been on retainer, the more they'll likely know about the company and the more they can tell you. And *are* they on retainer? Or are they just one of many firms that get paid only if they place someone?

Who is your contact at the company?

Is it the person who is actually doing the hiring or just someone in the Human Resources department?

How many people have you placed there?

Is a written, detailed job description available?

Why is this job available? Is this a new position? Was it created as part of a new project, division, or strategy?

New positions imply growth. Any company growing now may well be one you want to work for!

If it's not a new position, what happened to the person who previously held it?

If they were fired, can you tell me why? If they were promoted, where did they end up?

To whom would I be reporting? What can you tell me about him or her?

How many people would be reporting to me? What can you tell me about them?

What kind of a maelstrom are you diving into? It may be hard to get a truthful answer to this question from the head-hunter, and harder still from the hiring manager, but don't walk blindly into a department that's heading for a meltdown.

How long has this job been open?

How many candidates has the interviewer already seen?

If the job has been open for months, and the interviewer has already seen dozens of candidates, no explanation is positive: The interviewer is fishing for someone who doesn't exist, can't make up his mind, or keeps changing the description of what he's seeking. Or else the job, company, or people are so scary that candidates wind up running for the hills. Whichever the case, the longer the job has been open, the more suspicious you should be . . . and the more probing questions you should ask.

How long do you think the interview process for this job will take?

You know what I'm making and what I'd like to make. You know the kind of overall package I'm seeking. Do you foresee any problems with the company meeting my needs?

Would the recruiter send you on an interview with a company offering significantly less than he knows you require? Doubtful. But there's no reason for you to wait to ask this question until after you've already gone through a series of interviews at the company . . . only to discover that, whoops!, he did just that.

Is the person with whom I'm interviewing the decision maker? If she isn't, who is?

Is the interviewer my potential boss?

If so, you won't necessarily approach the interview itself any differently, but you will certainly spend more time gauging the chemistry between you and him.

What can you tell me about the culture of the company? Is there anything specific I should avoid doing or discussing?

This is information that is invaluable—a "heads up" that may put you head and shoulders above the candidates who inadvertently say or do the wrong thing.

Before you set up an interview for me, could I meet with some of the other people you've already placed at this company?

Not all recruiters will welcome this question or respond positively to it. It delays their ability to get you in the door, a delay that may conceivably cost you the job (and them a commission). So I would consider asking this question only if other answers have caused you to wonder whether you want to interview there at all.

How integral to the success of the company is the department I'd be joining?

A positive answer is especially important to the more ambitious among you. If the department is the vital hub of the whole operation, getting hired may thrust you into the middle of the action and greatly increase your chances to be seen, evaluated, appreciated, and promoted. On the other hand, a support department may be less pressured and less hectic . . . but less rewarding, too.

Is there anything else I need to know that would either doom my chances or help me ace the interview?

It's the last question you should ask them. Give them one more chance to offer that magic elixir that will turn your interview experience into gold.

WHY YOU SHOULD AVOID HUMAN RESOURCES

There aren't many career books that will advise you to make a beeline for the Human Resources department of a company you've targeted. In fact, most, if not all, will tell you to avoid it like the plague if at all possible. What have these poor (formerly) personnel people done to generate such animosity?

Nothing, really. I'm sure many of them are very nice people who do their jobs very well. The problem is that their jobs have little to do with actually getting *you* a job. They are *not* seeking candidates to interview and hire; they are trying to maximize the number they can *eliminate*. They are the screeners, the people who sift the sands of the known employment universe to discard the unqualified, the overqualified, the underqualified, and the "mis-qualified." They can say no. And they do. A lot. But they *can't* say *yes*.

In addition to not being able to actually offer you anything more than coffee or tea (and maybe an IQ or drug test), the staffers in many Human Resources departments may have (surprisingly) little idea about what hiring managers really want in job applicants. The more technical or specialized the field, the truer this statement.

I know of a Human Resources Director who recommended a candidate for whom English was a second—and not very *good*—language for the top editorial post on a major association magazine. Another passed along a candidate who got 55 out of 100 on a spelling test for a proofreading position. Still another recommended someone for a Vice President of Finance position whose resume was filled with rather obvious and easily discovered lies.

At many organizations, even hiring managers make it a point to go around their Human Resources departments—bringing candidates in, interviewing them, and only *then* passing them along so Human Resources can take care of the paperwork.

Make it easier for the hiring manager to do just that. Make every effort to get in touch with him or her directly, preferably by dropping the name of a "friend of a friend."

If you *must* go through Human Resources (and sometimes, despite your best efforts, you *will*), you can't ignore their power: They're the only ones who can get you to the next level—the real interview. So it certainly would behoove you to make friends with them and use them in whatever way you can.

Staffers in the best departments can and do know more than they are sometimes given credit for. They know the company, they may know something about the job, and they probably know whom you'll be working for, whom you'll be working with, and whom you'll be supervising. They can steer you in the right direction and help you appreciate the culture you're about to confront.

The Personnel Manager at a major magazine publisher I worked for was such a veteran. She knew where all the bodies were buried . . . and who should join them. With her help and input, I became the first person without previous magazine experience ever hired at that company. I paid her back by not only becoming the youngest sales manager in the company's history, but doing it more quickly than anyone had ever done it.

Nevertheless, you will probably not go wrong if you presume that the Human Resources person conducting a screening interview has no time to become your best friend, knows little or nothing about the job you so desperately want, and knows even less about the hiring manager.

But it's worth asking many of the same questions you would ask a recruiter or employment agency, and a few others. (As always, these are *not* in any order.):

What are your recruiting plans this year?

How is your recruiting going?

In other words, are they expanding? Do people want to work there? A talkative assistant might blithely confide to you that it's been difficult for them to find qualified candidates. That failure should give you pause: What do those candidates—the ones seemingly giving this company a wide berth—know that you don't?

What's a key thing about your company you'd like potential new hires to know?

What are the company's priorities? If the answer is a series of numbers—grosses, sales, profits, ratios—you've just discovered your place in the pecking order: the bottom line. Personally, I'd value (and survive!) at a company that talked more about teamwork, the accomplishments of its people, or its sense of social responsibility. Make sure the company values what *you* do, or it will be an unwieldy fit—and probably a short stay.

> **Tell me some of the particular skills or attributes that you want in the candidate for this position.**

The answer should tell you how much your traits are valued by the company. With this information, you can underline those traits you possess at the close of this interview—to end it on a strong note—as well as during the hiring interview.

> **Given my qualifications, skills, and experience, do you have any concerns about my ability to become an important member of this company?**

Probably not—if you didn't meet the summary of qualifications forwarded to Human Resources, you wouldn't be talking to anyone. But it never hurts to ask a question designed to uncover hidden objections. (See Chapter 6 for a much fuller discussion of this topic and a number of additional questions.)

> **How quickly are you hoping to fill this position?**
>
> **Where are you in the decision-making process?**
>
> **How would you say I stack up against the other candidates you've interviewed?**
>
> **Can you tell me more about what I'd be doing on a daily basis?**
>
> **How would you describe the corporate culture?**
>
> **How would you characterize the company's overall management style?**

What can you tell me about the interviewer?

What can you tell me about my boss?

What can you tell me about the people with whom I'll be working?

What can you tell me about the people I'll be managing?

If you're going to be managing a significant number of people, it's unlikely you'd be forced to start in HR, but I've included this question here anyway.

Does the company have a mission statement or written philosophy? May I have a copy?

If not, consider the Chairman's message in the annual report the corporate mission statement.

Are there any challenges facing this department right now? (Your department, not HR.)

Do you have a written description of the position? I want to make sure I understand my duties and responsibilities and the results you expect me to achieve.

This is a good question to pose to the screening interviewer (and a great way to ask it). It will help you prepare to face the hiring manager. If a written description doesn't exist, ask the interviewer to tell you what she considers the primary functions of the job.

Watch out for job descriptions that are too general, too elaborate, or too far-fetched. That doesn't mean you shouldn't schedule an interview, but it does mean you have to ask some clarifying questions. Why do companies lay out such god-awful descriptions? Why doesn't the hiring manager take the time to more clearly define the role he wants you to play (and then tell those poor people in Human Resources so *they* can do a better job screening candidates)? It's a mystery.

What other positions at the company should this job prepare me for? Is that the career track my predecessors followed?

You don't want to blindly stumble into a dead-end job. So find out how you can expect to advance after you land this job. What happened to the person you would be replacing? Is he or she still with the company? If so, doing what?

Try to pursue this line of questioning without giving the impression that you can't wait to get *out* of a job you don't even *have* yet! If you ask questions like this in a completely nonthreatening manner, your ambition will be understood, even welcomed.

At the end of this chapter, I've included a more comprehensive list of questions to ask about the company, department, and position. Use it to craft your own list for Human Resources.

Am I overqualified?

This, of course, is a question you really should ask *yourself* before you go on *any* interview. It's essential to admit, at least to yourself, if you *are* seriously overqualified for a position. Many of you might think it's easier to get a job beneath your qualifications—to work as an accounting assistant when you've been a full-charge bookkeeper, to be a receptionist when you've been an office manager, to go back to sales after rising to sales manager.

It isn't. You may have more qualifications than the job requires, but you may no longer have the *specific* qualifications it *demands*. While you may have overseen a 20-person sales force and be known far and wide as an ace motivator, you will have trouble getting a job selling copy machines. Why? Because they don't *care* about your management and motivational credentials. Nor do they need them. They want to know how many copy machines you're capable of selling a month. And they *do* care that you've never sold one!

Employers may question the motivation of someone willing to "do almost anything." Will such an employee just show up, doing what's asked and little more? What about someone willing to work "for almost nothing"? To quote another cliché: You get what you pay for. And that's exactly what "almost nothing" is worth.

Especially in lower-level jobs, employers want people happy to be doing what they were hired to do, not constantly looking around and commenting how they could do the boss's job better than he could. The office manager wants to treat the receptionist as a receptionist, not someone who has been an office manager and may, indeed, know more than he does about running an office. Just as some managers worry about hiring underlings who they fear may one day outshine them, many people worry about hiring people for low-level jobs who have already done what their boss is doing. It's disconcerting and, to many, highly threatening.

QUESTIONS TO ASK YOUR PEERS (FUTURE COLLEAGUES)

If you actually find a way to talk with your potential peers (and in some companies, it is a normal part of the interviewing process), you will want to ask them many of the same questions you would ask a recruiter, keeping in mind that they will not necessarily be as forthcoming and may be wary of being *too* honest. Nevertheless, their input can be an invaluable part of your decision making.

Why did you decide to work here?

What were your expectations when you started here? Were they met? How have they changed?

What do you consider this company's (department's) strengths and weaknesses?

If you had to do it over again, would you work here?

What can you tell me about working for _____?

How long have you worked for him or her?

How would you characterize his or her management style?

How are your contributions to the organization measured? Does the company support you with ongoing training and education?

What do you know now that you wish you had known before you took your job?

How many hours a day do you usually work? Do you have to work weekends?

Do you consider this company to be an ideal employer? Why or why not?

YOU MAY BE SCREENED BY PHONE OR IN PERSON

Your "preinterview" with an employment agency, recruiter, headhunter, or Human Resources may be on the phone or in person.

Telephone screening is an effective tactic used by many interviewers. Some interviewers, however, rely on the strategy as a *primary* means of qualifying candidates. For many of these interviewers, the in-person interview is little more than an opportunity to confirm what they feel they've already learned on the phone.

Interviewers who typically fall into this category are entre-preneurs, CEOs, high-level executives, and others short on time and long on vision. Their guiding philosophy could be summed up as "I have a personnel problem to solve, and I don't plan to waste my valuable time talking in person to anybody but the very best."

A telephone screener is also often the dominant inter-viewer at small- to mid-sized companies where no formal Human Resources (or Personnel) department exists or where such a department has only recently been created. The primary objective of the telephone screener is to *identify reasons to* **re-move** *you from active consideration* **before** *scheduling an in-person meeting.*

Among the common reasons for abrupt removal from the telephone screener's short list: evidence that there's a disparity between your resume and actual experience; poor verbal com-munication skills; or lack of required technical skills.

If you are expecting a call (or calls) from telephone screen-ers, make sure family members know how to answer the phone. Hint: A sullen "Huh?" from your teenage son or brother is not the best way. And by all means avoid cutesy answering ma-chine tapes. ("Hi!" [giggle, giggle] "We're upstairs getting our groove on!" [giggle, snort] "So leave a message, dude.")

What could be better than answering questions from the comfort of your own home?

For starters, conducting a telephone interview has cost you two valuable tools you have to work with during in-person in-terviews: eye contact and body language. You're left with your skills, the facts on your resume, and your ability to communicate verbally.

Don't be discouraged. *Always* project a positive image through your voice and your answers. Don't overdo it, but don't let the telephone be your undoing either. If your confidence is flagging, try smiling while you listen and speak. Sure, it might look silly, but it works. I also like to stand, even walk around, during a telephone interview. It seems to simultaneously calm me down and give me more energy.

You have a right to be prepared for any interview. Chances are, the interviewer will call you to set a time for the telephone interview. However, if she wants to plow right into it as soon as you answer the phone, there's nothing wrong with asking if she could call back at a mutually agreeable time. You need to prepare your surroundings for a successful interview.

Next to the phone, you'll want to have a copy of your resume (which you've quickly reviewed), the cover letter you sent to that company, a list of questions *you've* prepared for *them,* a notepad, your research materials on that company, and a glass of water. You will also want to have already answered nature's call (since you surely don't want to excuse yourself in the middle of the interview) and placed a "Do Not Disturb" sign on your door, so family members or roommates don't interrupt. Needless to say, you never want to put the interviewer on hold for any reason.

DID THE INTERVIEWER DIAL A WRONG NUMBER?

The main rule most telephone screeners follow (or are taught to follow) is *not* to extend an offer for a face-to-face interview to anyone they feel is not well suited to the position or the company. If the phone interview has led them to this conclusion, there are two ways they will try to wrap up. The first is to let you down easy:

> *"Mike, I really appreciate your taking the time to talk about your background with me today. You've given me a lot to think about. You should know, though, that this is a very competitive position and*

> *that we'll be talking to a lot of people over the next week or so.*
>
> *"I think the way I'd like to leave this is that if we feel there's the possibility of a good match for this position or for any other opening, we can get back in touch with you at this number. Does that make sense?"*

There is another school of thought about the best way to conclude a screening conversation—the direct approach (which I personally favor). It could go something like this:

> *"Mike, I've listened carefully to what you've told me today, and I have to be honest with you—I don't think we have a good match here. We're going to have to take a pass this time around."*

What can you do to fight off either of these brush-offs?

In the first instance, the door has been left at least a little ajar. So a truly aggressive rejoinder is not called for. Nevertheless, you cannot allow the screener to hang up without finding some way to actually get *in* that door, to make him or her reconsider. Here's one way to accomplish that:

> *"Mr. Billingsly, I appreciate how hectic your sched-ule is, but I think we would both benefit if you could spare me some time to meet in person. May I call your secretary to schedule a brief 15-minute meeting with you next week?"*

If the interviewer is a soft touch, the very fact that you resisted his attempt to brush you off might make him relent. Even a tougher interviewer, though, would be impressed with the confident tone you struck ("we would both benefit"), the understanding you demonstrated ("hectic schedule"), and the modest request you made ("15 minutes").

In the second instance, you have to be more aggressive because the interviewer is being more aggressive. Try something like the following:

> *"Mr. Herman, I'm surprised to hear you say that. I must have done a poor job communicating the credentials that make me perfect for this job and my enthusiasm for it. We obviously need to meet in person to discuss this more. Which would be better for you, Monday at 10 or Tuesday at 3?"*

Did it ever occur to you that Herman's aggressive brush-off could be a conscious strategy, an attempt to gauge how you will respond to such outright rejection? If you're applying for a sales position, I wouldn't be at all surprised if it were. And if you just rolled over and accepted his brush-off, then the interviewer would conclude you *couldn't* handle rejection (a huge factor in sales) and *wouldn't* be right for the job after all. Respond to an aggressive brush-off by being equally aggressive. The alternative is unappetizing—to hang up and move on to the next interview.

Many human resources and personnel professionals fall into a different category—human screens. For them, interviewing is not simply a once-a-quarter or once-a-month event, but rather a key part of their daily job descriptions. They meet and interview many people, and are more likely than a telephone screener to consider an exceptional applicant for more than one opening within the organization.

A primary objective of a human screen is to *develop a strong group of candidates for managers* (the third kind of interviewer) *to interview in person*. To do this, of course, they must fend off many applicants and callers, a daunting task, because the human screen or the department in which he works is often the only contact provided in employment advertisements.

Among the most common reasons for removal from a human screen's "hot" list are: lack of the formal or informal qualifications outlined in the organization's job description; sudden changes in hiring priorities and/or personnel requirements; poor performance during the in-person interview itself; or inaction due to uncertainty about your current status or contact information. That last reason is more common than you might imagine. Human screens are constantly swamped with phone calls, resumes, and unannounced visits from hopeful applicants. Despite their best efforts, they sometimes lose track of qualified people.

Human screens excel at separating the wheat from the chaff. Because they are exposed to a wide variety of candidates on a regular basis, they usually boast more face-to-face interviewing experience than other interviewers. They may be more likely to spot inconsistencies or outright lies on resumes, simply because they've seen so many over the years that they know when a candidate's credentials for a given position don't quite pass the "smell test."

And while interviews with a telephone screener or the hiring manager may be rushed because of their hectic schedules, human screens are often able to spend a comparatively long amount of time with particularly qualified candidates.

However, these interviewers often do not have direct knowledge of the day-to-day requirements of the job to be filled. They have formal summaries, of course, but they often don't possess the same first-hand familiarity with the skills, temperament, and outlook necessary for success on the job. Typically one step away from the action, they're reliant on job postings and experience summaries (often composed by managers).

If those formal outlines are imperfectly written, and if human screens receive no direct input from supervisors on the kinds of people they're seeking, you may be passed through the process even though you're not particularly qualified (or eliminated even though you are).

Not surprisingly, human screens often react with a puzzled look if others ask them to offer their gut reaction to a particular candidate. Because they're generally operating at a remove from the work itself, they often prefer quantifying their assessments of candidates in hard numbers: Either the candidate *does* have three years of appropriate experience, or she *doesn't*. Either she *has* been trained in computer design, or she *hasn't*. Of course, this analysis may overlook important interpersonal issues.

DON'T BELIEVE EVERYTHING YOU READ

And don't believe everything company representatives tell you. Just as employees have been known to "forget" a job when writing their resume and slightly exaggerate their responsibilities, employers have been known to tell attractive candidates what *they* want to hear. *"Need your space and independence? Like to work in a freewheeling, open kind of atmosphere? Hey, that's us!"* Except, unfortunately, for the one Neanderthal who just happens to be . . . your prospective boss.

It happened to my wife. At one time we both wound up working for the same magazine publishing company, though we experienced totally different corporate cultures.

One reason was because I was in corporate headquarters (New York), and she was based in an outpost (Chicago). I had 400 people around me, including all the major executives and the two owners. She had seven other salespeople and a secretary around her. Whatever answers she got about the corporate culture would have born little resemblance to the reality she lived.

She also had one of the above "Neanderthal" bosses, who, again, bore no resemblance to anyone else I ever worked with or for at that company. As a result, while I was in an environment that allowed me a lot of freedom and the ability to pretty much set my own priorities and schedule, she was virtually a prisoner of the time sheet and the object of frequent bullying rants.

Companies sometimes consciously misstate job requirements in their advertisements so as to attract, they believe, the higher end of the applicant pool.

If their gut feeling is that the job requires two years of experience, they may say three are required, expecting a higher grade of queries. They may also believe that the few people who do contact them with only two years of experience are likely to be more motivated than the average applicant.

This is called an "enhanced excluder," a means of setting the bar *slightly* higher than they need to, knowing they can always ignore the standards they've set for the right candidate. Some companies use this method almost as a preinterviewing technique, a way to see which applicants try to get around the announced requirements . . . and how compelling a case they can make for themselves.

If candidates absolutely, positively *have* to have particular technical expertise, that requirement should be prominently and specifically featured in the advertisement. This sounds self-evident, but you'd be surprised at the number of hiring managers I've spoken to who *don't* specify particular skills they're seeking . . . and then complain about the experience levels of the candidates they interview. Ambiguous statements like "good computer skills" don't help an employer attract the skilled people it's seeking. And they certainly don't help *you* figure out whether you're qualified for the position!

AN ORGANIZED LIST OF QUESTIONS

Here is a comprehensive list of questions to ask about the company, department, and/or job. Some may have already been answered through your research; some may be pertinent for the Human Resources screener; some may be more pertinent for the hiring manager. In any case, add them to your list of smart questions!

QUESTIONS ABOUT THE COMPANY

Who owns the company?

What are your leading products or services? What products or services are you planning to introduce in the near future?

What are your key markets? Are they growing?

Will you be entering any new markets in the next couple of years? Which ones and via what types of distribution channels?

What growth rate are you currently anticipating? Will this be accomplished internally or through acquisitions?

How many employees work for the organization? In how many offices? In this office?

Are you currently planning any acquisitions?

What has been your layoff history in the last five years? Do you anticipate any cutbacks in the near future and, if you do, how will they impact my department or position?

What major problems or challenges have you recently faced? How were they addressed? What results do you expect?

What is your share of each of your markets?

Which other companies serving those markets pose a serious threat?

What is your hiring philosophy?

What are your plans and prospects for growth and expansion?

What are your goals in the next few years?

What is your ranking within the industry? Does this represent a change from where it was a year or a few years ago?

Please tell me about your own tenure with this company.

What do *you* like best about this company? Why?

QUESTIONS ABOUT THE DEPARTMENT

Could you explain the organizational structure of the department and its primary functions and responsibilities?

To whom will I be reporting? To whom does he or she report?

With which other departments would I work most closely?

How many people work exclusively in this department?

What problems is this department facing? What are its current goals and objectives?

QUESTIONS ABOUT THE JOB

Is a written job description available?

What kind of training should I expect and for how long?

Please tell me more about your training programs. Do you offer reimbursement for job-related education? Time off?

How many people will be reporting to me?

Is relocation an option, a possibility, or a requirement?

How did this job become available? Was the previous person promoted? What is his or her new title? Was the previous person fired? Why?

Would I be able to speak with the person who held this job previously?

Could you describe a typical day in this position?

How long has this position been available?

Is there no one from within the organization who is qualified for this position?

Where will I be working? May I see my office/cubicle?

How advanced/current is the hardware and software I will be expected to use?

How much day-to-day autonomy will I have?

Does this job usually lead to other positions in the company? Which ones?

Please tell me a little bit about the people with whom I'll be working most closely.

QUESTIONS ABOUT THE NEXT STEP

How many other candidates have you interviewed?

How many more will you be interviewing before you expect to make a decision?

Before you're able to reach a hiring decision, how many more interviews should I expect to go through and with whom?

With whom will I be meeting next (names and job titles)?

What issues are important to each of them?

What are they like?

Are they amiable, laid back, hard charging? You want to be ready for the personality you're going to face. Won't you act differently with a fire-breathing sales type than you would with a mild-mannered bean counter? Of course you would. Additionally, you wouldn't want to overemphasize your computer expertise with the guy who is computer illiterate; it would just make him feel inferior . . . to a potential subordinate.

What are their ages and family situations?

You would not ask this question of a hiring manager or anyone else with direct input into the hiring decision. Since *they* can't, by law, ask you these types of questions, you would (I hope) be careful to avoid such personal questions yourself. But even though it's a small risk, I think it's worth it to get whatever such information you can from the lower-level interviewers. The more you know, the more you can prepare.

How long have they been with the company?

If the interviewer is middle-aged and in a middle-management position at a smaller company, he's either not the most ambitious person you ever met or has "risen to the level of his incompetence." You may want to make him feel secure—by not coming on too strong—since he's probably aware he isn't moving any higher up the corporate ladder.

On the other hand, if you're interviewing with a 27-year-old vice president who clearly seems destined for better things (and higher levels), you'll want to convince her that you're someone she'll want to bring along for the ride, someone who can perhaps make her own rise quicker or easier.

You may not be able to find out the answers to all or even most of these personal questions, but you will certainly get helpful answers to some. *Whatever* you learn will be more than you knew before!

Based on the answers you receive to these kinds of questions, try to create a model of the person with whom you'll be meeting: what she looks like, what makes her smile, what makes her angry, how she deals with stress, what seems important to her, what she'd laugh off.

Using this admittedly hypothetical "pseudo-interviewer," picture yourself actually in the interview with her. Answer her questions. Ask yours. Counter her objections. Ask for the job! Even if the eventual reality bears little or no resemblance to the model you've constructed, doing this exercise has got to make you better prepared than just walking in cold.

All the research, assessment, and preparation is over. It's time for the real thing—your interview with the hiring manager.

Questions to Ask
Your New Boss

The hiring manager may not be the person for whom you will be working, but he or she probably will be. Even where others have strong input, most companies still allow managers to hire their own staff, within certain parameters. He is probably a supervisor who has chosen (or is required) to shoehorn in-person interviews into his busy workdays. (In smaller companies especially, the president may be the ultimate decision maker, even if you won't be reporting to her.) A manager who has worked with a number of previous employees who held the same position brings a unique perspective to the proceedings.

What's different about interviewing with the hiring manager as opposed to the time spent with a recruiter or headhunter or even Human Resources? This is the person you actually have to impress, the only one who can say those magic words, "*You're hired. When can you start?*" This is the person you have to be careful with.

The hiring manager's primary objective is to *evaluate your skills and measure your personal chemistry on a firsthand basis.* These interviewers want to get to know everything they can about the people with whom they'll be working closely. (As we've seen, the telephone screener, by contrast, may well be an entrepreneur who delegates heavily and interacts only intermittently with new hires. And the human screen usually has nothing to do with the day-to-day operation of the company.)

Common reasons for being dropped from a hiring manager's "hot" list include: lack of personal chemistry or rapport; poor performance during the interview itself; and her assessment that, although you may be qualified and personable, you would simply not fit in well with the team.

Many hiring managers have an excellent intuitive sense of who will (and won't) perform the job well and achieve a good fit with the rest of the work group. On the other hand, it sometimes comes as a surprise to applicants that excellent supervisors can be less than stellar interviewers. But a great many managers lack any formal training in the art of interviewing.

It is this type of interviewer who is most likely to interpret the interview as an opportunity to "get to know" more about you, rather than to require specific answers to questions about your background, experience, outlook on work, and interpersonal skills.

THE HIRING INTERVIEW

Your first interview with the person who will manage your prospective position is not likely to be a walk in the park. You may be stepping out of the range of the experience and interviewing talent of the Human Resources professional and into unknown territory.

And you could wander there for a while.

Why? Experienced interviewers are trained to stay in charge of the interview, not let it meander down some dead-end, nonproductive track. There is a predictability to the way they conduct interviews, even if they utilize different techniques.

On the other hand, the hiring manager is sure to lack some or all of the screening interviewer's knowledge, experience, and skill—making him an unpredictable animal.

A majority of corporate managers don't know what it takes to hire the right candidate. Few of them have had formal training in conducting interviews of any kind. To make things worse, most managers feel slightly less comfortable conducting the interview than the nervous candidate sitting across their desks from them!

For example, a manager might decide you are not the right person for the job without ever realizing that the questions he or she asked were so ambiguous, so off the mark, that even the perfect candidate could not have returned the right answers. No one monitors the performance of the interviewer. And the candidate cannot be a mind reader. So more often than is necessary, otherwise perfectly qualified candidates walk out the door for good . . . simply because *the manager* failed at the interview!

FOILING THE INEPT INTERVIEWER

But that doesn't have to happen to you. You can—and should—be prepared to put your best foot forward, no matter what the experience or expertise of the manager interviewing you.

You'll be a step ahead of the game (and the other candidates) if you realize at the outset that the interviewer is after more than just facts about your skills and background. He is waiting for something more elusive to hit him, something he may not even be able to articulate: He wants to feel that, somehow, you "fit" the organization or department.

Knowing what you're up against is half the battle. Rather than sit back passively and hope for the best, you can help the unskilled interviewer focus on how your unique skills can directly benefit—"fit"—the department or organization by citing a number of specific examples. And by asking a number of smart questions.

What other unusual problems could you face during an interview?

THE "IT'S ALL ABOUT ME" INTERVIEWER

Bob thinks he's a pretty good interviewer. He has a list of 15 questions he asks every candidate—same questions, same order, every time. He takes notes on their answers and asks an occasional follow-up question. He gives candidates a chance to ask questions. He's friendly, humorous, and excited about working at Netcorp.com. As he tells every candidate . . . in detail . . . for *hours.* Then he wonders why only a small fraction of his hires pan out.

I've never really understood the interviewer who thinks telling the story of his or her life is appropriate. Why do some interviewers do it? Partly nervousness, partly inexperience, but mostly because they have the mistaken notion they have to sell *you* on the company, rather than the other way around. There *are* occasions when this *may* be necessary—periods of low unemployment, a glut of particular jobs and a dearth of qualified candidates, a candidate who's so desirable the interviewer feels, perhaps correctly, that he or she has to outsell and outbid the competition.

Under most circumstances, as I instruct novice interviewers in *Ask the Right Questions, Hire the Right People* (this book from the other side of the desk), *you* should be expected to carry the conversational load, while the interviewer sits back and decides if he or she is ready to buy what you're selling.

Is it to your benefit to find yourself seated before Mr. Monologue? You might think so. After all, while he's waxing poetic about the new cafeteria, you don't have to worry about inserting your other foot in your mouth. No explaining that last firing or why you've had four jobs in three months. Nope, just sit back, relax, and try to stay awake.

But I don't believe Mr. M. is doing you any favors. Someone who monopolizes the conversation doesn't give you the opportunity *you* need to "strut your stuff." You may want to avoid leaving a bad impression, but I doubt you want to leave *no* impression at all. As long as you follow the advice in this book and, especially, this chapter, you should welcome the savvy interviewer who asks the open-ended, probing questions *he* needs to identify the right person for the job—the same questions *you* need to convince him it's *you*.

THE "OUT OF IT" INTERVIEWER

Yes, interviewers have been known to be drunk, stoned, or otherwise incapacitated. Some have spent virtually the entire time allotted to a candidate speaking on the phone or browsing E-mail. Others have gone off on tirades about interoffice disputes or turf wars.

If the interviewer treats you with such apparent indifference before you're even hired, how do you expect him to act once you *are* hired?

There *is* a boss out there willing to treat you with the same respect she would expect from you; it's just not this one. Move on.

TIME TO GET UP CLOSE AND PERSONAL

There are a number of styles and guiding philosophies when it comes to person-to-person interviews. The overall purpose, of course, is to screen you out if you lack the aptitudes (and attitudes) the company is looking for.

Although experienced interviewers may use more than one strategy, it's essential to know which mode you're in at any given point *and* what to do about it. Here's a summary of the methods and objectives of the most common approaches.

THE BEHAVIORAL INTERVIEW

Your conversations with the interviewer will focus almost exclusively on your past experience as he tries to learn more about how you have already behaved in a variety of on-the-job situations. Then he will attempt to use this information to extrapolate your future reactions on the job.

How did you handle yourself in some really tight spots? What kinds of on-the-job disasters have you survived? Did you do the right thing? What were the repercussions of your decisions?

Be careful what you say. Every situation you faced was unique, so be sure to let the interviewer in on specific limitations you had to deal with. Did you lack adequate staff? Support from management? The latest software? If you made the mistake of plunging in too quickly, say so and admit that you've learned to think things through. Explain what you'd do differently the next time around.

Remember: Those interviewers using a behavioral interview are trying to ensure you can really walk the walk, not just talk the talk. So leave out the generalizations and philosophizing, and don't get lost in the details. In other words, just tell them the problems you faced, the actions you took, and the results you achieved, without exaggeration.

Which is why composing three or four "stories"—actual experiences that illustrate your most important skills or qualifications—is important preparation. Just make sure to structure them in "Problem-Solution-Action" format.

THE TEAM INTERVIEW

Today's organizational hierarchies are becoming flatter. That means that people at every level of a company are more likely to become involved in a variety of projects and tasks, including interviewing *you*.

The team interview can range from a pleasant conversation to a torturous interrogation. Typically, you will meet with a group, or "team," of interviewers around a table in a conference room. They may be members of your prospective department or a cross section of employees from throughout the company. (A slightly less stressful variation is the tag—team approach, in which a single questioner exits and is followed by a different questioner a few minutes—or questions—later.) Rarely will you be informed beforehand to expect a team interview.

The hiring manager or someone from Human Resources may chair an orderly session of question-and-answer, or he may turn the group loose to shoot questions at you like a firing squad. When it's all over, you'll have to survive the assessment of every member of the group.

Some hiring managers consult with the group after the interview for an evaluation of your performance. Others determine their decision using group consensus. The good news is that you don't have to worry that the subjective opinion of just one person will determine your shot at the job. If one member of the group thinks you lacked confidence or came across as arrogant, others in the group may disagree. The interviewer who leveled the criticism will have to defend her opinion to the satisfaction of the group—or be shot down herself.

A group of people is also more likely (but not guaranteed) to ask you a broader range of questions that may uncover and underline your skills and expertise. Just take your time, and treat every member of the team with the same respect and deference you would the hiring manager.

If you face a series of separate interrogations with a variety of interviewers and are hit with many of the same questions, be sure to vary your answers. Cite different projects, experiences, successes, and even failures. Otherwise, when they meet to compare notes, you'll come off as a "Johnny One Note."

THE STRESS INTERVIEW

Formal qualifications are important, but in some jobs, the emotional demands, sudden emergencies, and breakneck pace of work can be downright intimidating—not once in a while, but every day. Even a candidate who knows all the technical moves may wilt under the glare of an etiquette-challenged boss or crumble when inheriting a surrealistically compressed deadline.

When you're interviewing for such a position, whether you're seeking a job as a stockbroker, an air traffic controller, or a prison guard, an interviewer may feel it's almost meaningless to determine if you are capable of performing the job under the *best* conditions. He may well try to assess how you will do under the very *worst* conditions. And that's where the stress interview comes in.

Anyone who's been through one of these never forgets it. A common enough question in this setting could sound gruff or rude, which is exactly how it's supposed to sound. Rather than a pleasant, *"So, tell me about yourself,"* a stress interviewer may snarl (literally), *"So, why the hell should I hire you for anything?"*

How do you know you're facing a stress interview? Here are some techniques an interviewer may use:

- He ridicules everything you say and questions why you're even interviewing at his company.

- He says nothing when you walk into the room . . . and for five minutes afterwards . . . then just stares at you after you answer his first question.

- She keeps you waiting past the scheduled time, then keeps looking at her watch as you answer questions.

- She stares out the window and seems to be completely uninterested in everything you have to say.

- He challenges every answer, disagrees with every opinion, and interrupts you at every turn.

- He doesn't introduce himself when you walk in, just hits you with a tough question.

- She takes phone calls, works on her computer, and/or eats lunch as you interview.

- You may be seated in a broken chair, directly in front of a high-speed fan, or next to an open window . . . in the dead of winter.

If you are subjected to a stress interview, you may well question seeking a job with a company that utilizes such techniques. If they think insulting and belittling you during the interview are effective techniques, what's their management philosophy— gruel at nine, thumbscrews at two?

Don't confuse a stress interview with a *negative* interview. In the latter, the interviewer merely stresses the negative aspects of the job at every opportunity. He may even make some up: *"Would you have any problem cleaning the toilets every Saturday morning?"* or *"Is three hours of daily overtime a problem for you?"*

THE CASE INTERVIEW

> *"You're dealing with a publishing client. His printer just called and said the biggest book of the year had a typo on the spine. A bad typo. More than 100,000 books have already been printed. What should he do?"*

There's nothing quite like the terror of the hypothetical question. Especially when it is a product of the interviewer's rich imagination. It's your signal that you are about to undergo an increasingly popular type of interview—the case (or situational) interview. If you are seeking a job at a consulting firm, law firm, or counseling organization, you should expect to confront this type of interview.

The premise is sound: Present the candidate with situations that might, hypothetically, occur on the job, in order to gauge the degree to which he or she demonstrates the traits that will lead to success. It's hard, if not impossible, for you to prepare for these kinds of questions beforehand, which means you have to analyze an unfamiliar problem and develop a strategy to solve it, right then and there.

What most interviewers want to see is a combination of real-world experience, inspired creativity, and the willingness to acknowledge when more information or assistance is in order. (Many interviewers will pose hypothetical questions designed to smoke out people who find it difficult to reach out to other team members for help.) They want to understand how you approach a problem, the framework within which you seek a solution, and the thought process you utilize.

You will have to devote a great deal of thought to each of these questions. Here are some tips for confronting a case interview:

- Take notes on the problem that's presented. Ask questions about the details. Be aware that not all information is pertinent to the solution. (That wily interviewer!)

- Avoid generalizations. The interviewer will want to hear concrete steps that will lead to a solution, not your philosophy of how to approach the problem.

- Don't get lost in the details. The interviewer wants to see how you approach the broad problem, so set your sights on the most important factors.

- Ask questions.

- Share your thoughts—out loud. That's really what the interviewer wants to hear.

- Resist the urge for speed; take your time. The more complicated the problem, the more time you're *expected* to take.

- There's nothing wrong with a creative approach, but it should always be in a logical framework.

- Ask questions!

While case interviews are geared to upper-echelon candidates, candidates for many different kinds of jobs may be given the opportunity to "walk the walk" (show what they can actually do on the job): Clerks may be given typing or filing tests; copy editors given minutes to edit a magazine article or book chapter; a salesperson may be asked to telephone and sell a prospect; and a computer programmer may be required to create some code. The more technical the job, the more likely an interviewer will not simply take you at your word that you are capable of doing it.

THE BRAINTEASER INTERVIEW

As Microsoft interviewers have famously been known to ask, "How would you move Mt. Fuji?" The list of questions designed to assess how creatively you approach a problem, as opposed to the logical approach case interviews are designed to highlight, are virtually unlimited:

- How many oil wells are there in Texas?

- How many dentists are there in Poland?

- How would you build a better mousetrap?

Most of the same tips I gave you when approaching a case interview are still appropriate—take your time, ask pertinent questions, then talk through the approach you would take to answer the question.

WHAT THE INTERVIEWER WANTS TO SEE AND HEAR

What will the hiring manager be looking and listening for, right from the moment she meets you? Here's the advice *I* gave her in my book, *Ask the Right Questions, Hire the Best People*:

WHAT TO LOOK FOR: THE INITIAL GREETING

When you first encounter the candidate, silently ask yourself questions like the ones listed below. The more often you can answer "yes," the more likely it is that you've hooked up with a poised, confident candidate. Of course, no one is suggesting that confidence and social grace can compensate for a lack of ability in the workplace. But, in a perfect world, wouldn't you prefer to work with someone who meets all the formal qualifications . . . *and* has enough self-confidence to interact effectively with others?

- Did the candidate grip your hand firmly, avoiding both the "bone-crusher" and the "wet fish" approach?

- Did the candidate shake your hand with a sense of purpose?

- Did the candidate hold the shake for an appropriate period—neither too short nor too long? (Three shakes is sufficient.)

- Did the candidate use one hand? (A two-handed shake is usually regarded as a sign of over-familiarity at the outset of the first meeting, though there are some regional/cultural exceptions to this rule.)

● Did the candidate look you in the eye?

● Did the candidate smile?

● Did the candidate use your name when greeting you?

WHAT TO LOOK FOR: BODY LANGUAGE

Once the candidate takes a seat, you'll be doing the lion's share of the talking to begin the meeting. *After* you have put the person at ease by asking a few rapport-building questions, begin to monitor his or her gaze, physical posture, and general bearing. Use the questions below as a rough guideline, and make discreet notes as the interview moves forward. The more "yes" answers you record, the more comfortable (and, presumably, forthcoming) the person is likely to feel interacting with you.

● Does the candidate make appropriate intermittent eye contact with you—neither staring you down nor avoiding your gaze?

● Is eye contact broken only at natural points in the discussion, rather than suddenly, such as in the middle of an exchange?

● Is the candidate's mouth relaxed? (A tightly clenched jaw, pursed lips, or a forced, unnatural smile may indicate problems handling stress.)

● Are the candidate's forehead and eyebrows relaxed? (Ditto.)

● Does the candidate occasionally smile naturally?

- Does the person avoid nodding very rapidly for long periods of time while you're speaking? (This is shorthand for "Be quiet and let me say something now," and it is inappropriate in an interview setting.)

- Does the candidate move his or her hands so much or in such a weird manner that you actually notice? (Constant twitching of the fingers, or even worse, knuckle-cracking, may mean you're dealing with a person who simply can't calm down. Yes, an interview is an unsettling experience, but so are some of the tasks this person will have to perform on the job!)

- On a similar note, does the candidate avoid shuffling and tapping his or her feet?

- Is the candidate's posture good? (Chair-slumpers send an unfortunate silent message: "I'm not even trying to make a good impression." If you hire them, you may encounter that message on a daily basis.)

- Are the candidate's eyes usually gazing forward rather than darting all over the room?

- Is the candidate's head upright?

- Does the candidate tend to sit with crossed arms? (This may signal either a confrontational attitude or a sense of deep insecurity, neither of which is a great sign.)

- Does the person appear to be breathing regularly and deeply?

- Is the person's personal hygiene and grooming acceptable? (In other words, would you want to

sit next to this person during a long meeting?
Ask yourself: If the candidate won't make an
effort to clean up his or her act for a job
interview, what will the average workday be
like?)

WHAT TO LISTEN FOR

What the candidate says is certainly important, but so is *how* he
or she says it. Make circumspect written notes if you cannot answer "yes" to all of the following questions during the interview.
Three or more such notes during the course of a half-hour interview could indicate a problem with social skills.

- Does the candidate respond in a clear, compre-
  hensible, and confident tone of voice?

- Does the candidate avoid prolonged pauses in
  the middle of sentences?

- Is the candidate's speaking rhythm consistent
  and appropriate?

- Does the candidate avoid rambling answers?

- Does each of the candidate's answers have a
  clear concluding point, or do they all seem to
  just trail off into nothingness?

- Does the candidate avoid interrupting you?
  (Breaking in while a representative of a
  prospective future employer is speaking shows
  poor judgment and underdeveloped people
  skills.)

- Does the candidate take time to consider difficult questions before plunging in to answer
  them?

- Does the candidate ask for additional information or clarification when dealing with complex or incomplete questions?

- Does the candidate offer answers that are consistent with one another?

As you monitor nonverbal signals during the interview, bear in mind that physical actions and vocal delivery should support the answers the interviewee passes along. A candidate who assures you that he has what it takes to ride the ups and downs of a career in sales but looks pale and shell-shocked when you mention that you're interviewing other candidates, is sending two very different messages. The *lyrics* may be saying "I can handle rejection," but the *music* doesn't quite support that contention!

SMART INTERVIEW QUESTIONS FOR YOUR NEW BOSS

BASIC QUESTIONS

Revisit those basic questions you tried to answer through your research and those you asked the agency, recruiter, headhunter, or Human Resources department. If you've gotten satisfactory answers to them, you don't need to ask them again.

Whatever questions remain from this first list, ask them. Then add a few more:

Please explain the (department, division) company's organizational chart.

Can you give me a more detailed understanding of what my days might be like?

Are there specific challenges you are facing right now? Will I be in a position to help you overcome them?

What are the department's specific objectives for the next three months?

After you hear them, of course, you will do two things: Wrack your brain for specific examples from your experience or education that will convince him *you* can help him *reach* those goals. And ask more follow-up questions about how your job responsibilities will impact them.

Why three months? That's the length of your probable probation period.

You and (one of his important competitors) have many similar products (or offer similar services). What sets you apart from them? What's different about the way you do things? What's different about their corporate structure, mission, or philosophy?

How fast is the company growing? Is management happy with that rate, or do you have expansion plans in mind?

Growth can be a double-edged sword: Faster top-line growth (i.e., greater sales) could mean an opportunity to climb the career ladder faster than usual. It could also characterize a company that spends itself into oblivion trying to buy sales. (See "dot-com.")

What is the company's ranking within the industry? Does this position represent a change from where it was a few years ago?

You should already have some indication of the answer to this question from your initial research, particularly if the company is publicly owned. If you have some of this information, go ahead and build it into your question: *"I've read that the company has risen from fifth to second in market share in just the past three years. What are the key reasons for this dramatic success?"*

How do you see me working with each of the department heads?

How would my performance be measured in this position? How is the department's performance measured?

PROBING QUESTIONS

The previous basic questions, and many of those you asked during your research or while interviewing with an agency, recruiter, headhunter, or screening interviewer, are almost solely to fill in your overall portrait of the company as a whole. Once you have established in your own mind that you are truly interested in the company, you will want to ask detailed questions designed to elicit specific information about the department, the job, and the people:

What are the things you would most like to see changed in this (section, department, group, division, company)?

Are there plans for new products or services I need to know about?

When may I meet some of my potential colleagues (or subordinates). Are they part of the interviewing process here?

Including lower-level employees in the process proves that the company values its employees' opinion and realizes that just adding some stranger to the team by executive fiat isn't an effective way to show your employees how important they are to you. Nor does it do much for "team building" or any of those other corporate mantras that get thrown around.

How will you weight your subordinates' input with your own assessment of my candidacy?

Or (to the subordinates),

> **What kind of feedback does your boss expect you to give him? How much weight has he given it in the past?**

You can never be sure how much influence anyone has with the ultimate decision maker. I once interviewed at a company where a prospective new salesperson had to meet briefly with each of the seven sales managers, although the Vice President of Sales was the ultimate decision maker. Well, one of the two female managers (not the best or the brightest, I might add) was sleeping with the boss. I'm not sure how I would have ever found that out (it took me a few months at the company before the gossip reached my virginal ears), but it tends to emphasize the importance of treating everyone you meet with courtesy, respect, and professionalism. And that you can't easily discern who is going to be a key factor in your hiring . . . or your being passed over.

Even if the above lady wasn't sleeping with the boss, I guarantee if three or maybe even two of the sales managers had decided I "wouldn't fit in," that particular VP would have never hired me. Some bosses are more influenced than others, which leads to a good question if you're put in a similar situation:

> **Are there a lot of after-hours business events I will be expected to attend?**

> **How much travel should I expect to do in a typical month? Are there distinct periods of heavier travel?**

> **Do you have a lot of employees working flextime or telecommuting?**

Make sure you're careful not to imply this is one of your requirements, especially if the answer is a frosty, *"No. Everybody works nine to six, and I value punctuality."*

What has the turnover been in this department in the last couple of years?

Are you about to join a department that goes through sales-people like water through a hose? Who cares about the size of your raise and bonus if you won't be there in 60 days?

How many hours a week do you expect your star employees to put in? How much overtime does this position typically involve? How many week-ends a year would I be expected to work?

Please tell me a little bit about the people with whom I'll be working most closely."

I wish someone had told me about this question before my last job interview! The answer can tell you so many things: How good your potential colleagues really are at their jobs, how much you are likely to learn from them, and, most important, whether the hiring manager seems enthusiastic about his team.

A hiring manager usually tries to put on her best face during an interview, just like you. But catching the interviewer off guard with this question may give you a glimpse of the real feelings hiding behind her game face.

If she doesn't seem very enthusiastic about her current team, it may not be one you'd be particularly thrilled to join. This hiring manager may attribute little success, and perhaps a lot of headaches, to the people who work for her. Is that the kind of boss you want?

What is the department's budget?

Who is part of the planning process?

How much budgetary responsibility would I have?

I don't care if you're interviewing for the lowest position in the organization and the answer is, *"Are you kidding? You won't be able to buy paper clips without submitting a 6-part form and getting 14 signatures!"* This question shows that you are willing to take responsibility and understand the importance of doing so in order to move up the career ladder. Ask it.

Can you give me a better idea of the kinds of decisions I could make (or amounts of money I could spend) without oversight?

This is a question for anyone *above* the lowest level; it will help clarify what level of power you're *really* being handed and will give you greater insight into how centralized the company is. If you are at a fairly high level (manager, director, VP) and the answer is *"Oh, anything under $100; after that, you have to check with me,"* you may have just learned more than you really wanted to know about the limitations of your "power." In fact, at that supposed level, such an answer should send you running for the hills. I know *receptionists* who have more discretionary power!

Similarly, if you expect to have people reporting to you, your ability to hire and fire and your involvement in interviewing candidates for your own team should reflect your level of management, but it will also reflect the corporate structure and culture. I once worked for a medium-sized trade magazine publisher (400 people at headquarters, 100 more in regional offices) at which only the two owners had private secretaries. Everyone else, including the vice-presidents of sales, operations, production, circulation, and editorial, shared secretaries. Even after I reached management level, I was still sharing a secretary with one other manager and three salespeople!

What would you like to be able to say about your new hire one year from now?

What is the one thing I could do during my first three months on the job that would really get your attention?

How has this job been performed in the past?

What do you see as the key goals for the company during the next year? For my department? For this job?

How do you see my role evolving in the first two years? What would be the most logical areas for me to evolve into?

What do you think my biggest challenge will be if I start working for you?

Now, if a manager takes this question personally—interpreting it as *"What problems am I going to have with you?"*—that would tell me something about the manager. Perhaps he's a little self-centered? Perhaps he's prone to define *your* success by how well you get along with *him,* as opposed to how good a job you do?

On the other hand, she may blurt out, "Roberta," or some other name you soon find out is the "problem" member of the team. *Your* potential team.

Or it may just elicit a detailed monologue about competition, products, services, and/or the economy.

Whatever answer you get should give you a much better idea of how this interviewer thinks as a boss and what he sees as the focus of *his* job.

IT'S A MATTER OF STYLE

Even if you are comfortable with the job, the department, and the company—and have had most or all of your questions about them answered—never underestimate the importance of your boss's style, the corporate culture, and how you will mesh with both. The next two sections offer questions to make sure you achieve a comfy fit.

How would you describe your management style? Would you say that it's similar to others in the organization, or do you consider yourself a bit of a maverick?

When's the last time you got really angry at one of your subordinates? What was the cause? What did you do? Has anything similar happened since? Did you react differently?

In your experience, are there particular types of people you seem to work better with than others?

This is a not-so-veiled attempt to define yourself according to the attributes the manager cites, presuming, of course, that the type of person he describes isn't so remote from your own personality as to be laughable.

What particular traits do you value most in your subordinates?

Again, tell me what you want to hear, Mr. Manager, so I can tell you that I'm all that!

What kinds of people seem to succeed in this company? In this department? Working for you?

How do you define success?

Tell me about the last time one of your subordinates made a major mistake. What did he or she do? What did you do? How did that work out? What's your philosophy about mistakes?

How do you measure your own success?

What do you think your responsibility is to de-velop your people? Would you cite some examples of which you're particularly proud?

QUESTIONS ABOUT THE CULTURE, CHEMISTRY, FIT

What have *you* enjoyed most about working here?

What have you liked least?

What do *you* like best about this company? Why?

If the interviewer hems and haws a lot over this one, it may indicate that she doesn't really like the company at all.

If she's instantly enthusiastic, her answer should help sell you on her and the company.

The answer to this question can also give you a good sense of the values of the organization and the hiring manager. If she talks about nothing but products or how well her stock options are doing, it may indicate a lack of enthusiasm for the "people side" of the business.

What is your history with the company?

What's keeping you here now?

There are a lot of reasons to ask these questions, and to ask them early. You'll get a better feel for where the interviewer came from—up through the ranks (and the specific rungs along the way) or from outside the company, for example. How long he stayed at each position—is he a mover and shaker or a plodder? Whether he's been there long enough to give you an accurate feel of the culture.

The second question is an especially important one to ask of the person to whom you'll be reporting. Again, if the word "people" isn't part of her answer, what does that tell you about her leadership or management style? If the reasons are all financial, I would question his dedication to the core culture . . . and even whether I could count on him sticking around if another company dangled a bigger carrot in his face.

SEMI-CLOSING QUESTIONS

In the next chapter, we'll discuss in more detail how to identify hidden objections to your candidacy, how to confront them, and how to ask for the job offer—questions designed to "close the sale." But there are questions a step below (or before, if you prefer), what I've called "semi-closing questions," that are designed to indicate your strong interest in the position and elicit more of the information you need to weigh a potential offer:

> **Are there problems that keep you awake?**
>
> (Follow up) **What could I do to make you sleep better?**
>
> (Alternate) **How could I make your life easier?**
>
> **How will we work together to establish objectives and deadlines in the first months of this job?**

This is a nice way to find out how much input you will have or whether you're heading into a fait accompli—*"Glad you're here, Ron. Here's the plan for the next three months. Do it."*

> **Do my qualifications (experience, education, demeanor, outlook, spirit) remind you of another employee who succeeded at this job?**
>
> **What are your own goals for the coming year? How do you think I could specifically help you achieve them?**
>
> **If you were me, what are the three specific goals you would set for your first three months on the job?**

**What are three things that need immediate
attention?**

What skills are in short supply here?

**Are there other things you would like someone
to do that are not considered formal parts of the
job?**

What is the first problem I should tackle?

**What's the one thing I can do right at this job to
assure my success? What's the one thing that
would assure failure?**

**Would it be possible to talk with _____ (the
other department heads with whom I'd be
working, my team, my boss, some of my potential
colleagues/peers)?**

**Is there anything else you feel it is vital I know
about the company (department, job, your
expectations, etc.)?**

This is the last "nonclosing" question to ask. It is designed to
give the interviewer every opportunity to tell you anything else
he deems important.

A LITTLE KNOWLEDGE *IS* POWERFUL

The more research you've done, the easier it will be to incorporate what you've learned into great questions. In the same vein, the way you phrase a question can effectively show the interviewer how well you've been listening and absorbing his pearls of wisdom:

**The job seems to be in a state of flux. What's your
impression?**

Although your ad indicated that computer experience was the primary qualification, I get the impression from our talk so far that building a new team is your major concern. Do you agree?

Your company appears to be (team oriented, helter skelter, highly charged, serious, fun, etc.). Do you think that's an accurate assessment? If yes, can you tell me more about how that culture will impact how I work? If no, how would you describe it?

TIMING CAN BE EVERYTHING

If the absolutely perfect candidate walked in the door first thing Monday morning, I don't know any hiring managers who would simply hire him on the spot and tell everyone else to pound salt. Even if he was everything the manager could have ever asked for . . . and more! Why? Human nature: "I've got to see more than one candidate or I won't have anyone to compare him to. How can I just hire the first person who comes through the door? What would my boss think? That I'm too impulsive? Giving the interviewing process short shrift? A poor interviewer?"

The further along they are in the process, the better it probably is for you. Ever watch an ice skating competition? No one wants to go first, do they? (And the champ never does, does she? *Hmmm.*) Why? Even if the first skater were flawless, crafting a performance that demanded top marks, she'd never get them. If the judges gave *her* the highest marks, what would they do for one of the skaters who followed with an even *better* performance?

What if you're near the end of the process or even, ideally, *the very last person interviewed?* You are the person right in front of them—living, breathing, laughing, selling, questioning, impressing. Even if there *was* someone marginally better than you, that was hours, days, even *weeks* ago! Whatever impression that earlier candidate made, no matter how strong, is already fading. And there you are, saying all the right things, asking all the smart questions.

Remember what I said about how job descriptions are sometimes more fluid and changeable than employers would ever admit? By the time an interviewer gets near the end of the process, the job description has undoubtedly been altered by all those other candidates. Whatever unrealistic expectations he had at the beginning have been thrown out the window, because too many candidates proved to him they were wrong. He's measuring you by a completely new yardstick, one refined by all those other interviewees.

They've raised questions in his mind, too. Things he hadn't thought about before. So he's thinking differently not just about the job, but about the candidates.

Could one of those earlier candidates now be better qualified for the resulting job than you? Maybe. But if you make a sterling impression and say all the right things, the interviewer may never sift through that old stack of resumes or revisit his pages of notes. Out of sight, out of mind, when can *you* start?

CHAPTER

Questions to Close the Sale

At some point, it will dawn on you that you actually *want* this job. You may even have gotten the impression that the *interviewer* wants you to have the job. Or, at least, you think she does.

It's time to find out how real your chances are by asking "closing" questions—highly targeted questions designed to uncover the interviewer's (unstated) concerns, figure out where you are in the process, identify the competition, and, most important, ask for the job!

"IS THERE ANYONE ELSE . . . ?"

Salespeople know that one of the most deadly obstacles to closing a sale is talking to the wrong person. What good is a powerful, professional presentation that generates a series of enthusiastic "yes's" if the person you're selling lacks the authority to actually buy your product or service? While it may be important to get this person's recommendation, wouldn't *you* want to know you're actually interviewing with the person with the ability to say, *"Great! When can you start?"*

To forestall this waste of time and effort, top salespeople will often use a line like the following to qualify a prospect *before* they go into their spiel: *"Is there anyone else along with yourself who needs to be part of this discussion so a buying decision can be made today?"*

That's qualifying! Be ready to ask a similar question yourself:

Is there anyone else along with yourself who needs to be part of this interview so a *hiring* decision can be made today?

If the answer is "no," you can feel somewhat confident that this is the person you have to convince. Often, an employer will answer a question such as this by detailing the hiring process for you:

"Well, Jim, I'm ultimately going to be the one making the decision about whom to hire, but I'm going to have the top two or three candidates interview with _____ and _____ before I make the final cut."

Which would, of course, lead you to ask a whole series of other questions:

Will those other interviews be scheduled following this one?

Over what period of time will those other interviews take place?

How long a period have you set aside for interviews before you make a final decision?

At what point do you feel you will be making a final decision?

May I make appointments with those other executives immediately following this interview?

If you properly researched the interviewer and asked the right questions of the recruiter or headhunter with whom you're working (or the Human Resources person who preinterviewed you), you really should already know whether the person you're talking to is the ultimate decision maker. In an ideal world, of course. But the world these days is far from ideal. So ask this qualifying question early in the interview; it's important to know whether you're selling the Emperor . . . or merely one of his advisors.

UNCOVER HIDDEN OBJECTIONS

Salespeople also know (or quickly learn) that the key to any sale is filling their customers' needs . . . or at least convincing the customer that they *can* fulfill those needs. In order to get to that point, however, they may have to handle a series of objections, of which price is only one (though perhaps one that comes up more often than others). In order to *confront* these objections, they must be *identified*. Needless to say, not every buyer is blithely ready to volunteer the real reasons why he's unwilling to switch vendors (or reveal the magic words that will win his business).

So successful salespeople have developed detailed routines to elicit *hidden objections*—the unstated but real obstacles they must overcome to win the account. You must follow their lead. After all, you can't eliminate an objection you don't even know about.

Questions designed to clear your path are, by their very nature, a little intrusive, a little pushy, a little aggressive. But they must be asked:

Is there anything that is stopping you from offering me this job right now?

This is perhaps one of the more aggressive ways to phrase this question, but it certainly gets to the point. The interviewer may not bare his soul; he could answer, *"Yes, because you have three more interviews to go if you get past me!"* But at least you'll learn that much!

> **How do I compare with the others you've interviewed for this position?**

> **How many other people would you say are also serious candidates for this position? How do you see me stacking up against them?**

You can't really knock the competition, even if you wanted to (and you shouldn't want to), because no matter how much the interviewer tells you, you really won't know enough to do so. But it's essential that you know how many viable candidates there actually are and how the interviewer thinks you measure up. Invariably, rather than giving you a plethora of details about other candidates, you will hear something like, *"Well, you all have similar educations and experience, but there are some differences in computer skills. As you know, the ability to troubleshoot our system is a secondary but still very important part of the job description."* Hmmm, it might have been described as secondary in an ad, but clearly it's more important than you thought. Time to sell your computer skills, big time.

> **Are there any specific areas in which you believe my qualifications are lacking?**

> **Do you have any reservations about my ability to do this job?**

You're asking the interviewer for very specific feedback—lack of the pertinent degree, not quite enough experience, experience with a firm smaller than she would like, and so on. Her answer should enable you to spin your credentials so they mesh better with her requirements. Other versions of this same question might take slightly different tacks:

> **Do you have any concerns I haven't adequately addressed?**

> **Given my qualifications, skills and experience, do you have any concerns about my ability to become an important member of your team?**

> **Is there anything in my background, education, skills, or qualifications that concerns you?**

> **Is there anything else I can tell you that would help you make the decision to hire me?**

This is another variation that I like, because it craftily but directly implies your interest in the position, puts you in the position of "helping" rather than selling, and attempts to close the sale . . . all at the same time.

There is, of course, a not-so-fine line between appearing confident and being an arrogant boor. Adjust the level of aggressiveness to the tone of the interview. If you've done a good job establishing rapport with the interviewer and are having a comfortable, conversational interview, there's no reason to come off like a fire-breathing dragon when it's time to close the sale:

> **I think we've had an excellent talk, and I'm very interested in this position. Where do we go from here?**

or

> **When can I expect to hear from you? If you are unable to call me before then, would it be all right if I call you on _____?**

If the interviewer said he'd call Wednesday and doesn't, that's not a reason to lose sleep. Everything might be all right; a phone call the next morning might offer a credible excuse: *"Oh, Ron,*

I'm so sorry I couldn't get to you yesterday as promised, but I had to put out some raging fires." So arrange ahead of time to call him if you don't hear. You'll sleep better.

> **How am I doing? Do you think you will be recommending me to move on in the process?**

Hey, it was a successful catchphrase for former New York mayor Ed Koch, though I think it may come off a trifle too brazen (maybe even a little too glib).

Here are two questions that are the least aggressive, though still designed to make the interviewer give you the information you need:

> **What are the key criteria you're going to use to decide callbacks? How do I measure up, in your opinion?**
>
> **What are the next steps in the hiring process?**

There are few interviewers who, when asked either of these two questions, will not make it pretty clear to the candidates who aren't making the grade that the next step is to shake hands, smile, and go on to another company: *"How do you measure up, Brad? Well, I'm afraid you don't."*

Likewise, those viable candidates should be given a road map for the rest of the process—with whom they should meet next, how long the process should last, and how many other candidates are still in the running.

◼ SALESPEOPLE CAN BE MORE AGGRESSIVE

What if you're seeking a sales position? Since I've counseled *every* candidate to identify hidden objections through probing questions, ask closing questions, and, most important, ask for the offer, don't you think it's even *more* important for potential salespeople to aggressively seek answers . . . and the job?

You bet it is. Questions that may seem overly aggressive to an accounting major may appear positively mild to a fire-breathing salesperson. And most sales managers *expect* sales-people to be aggressive; it's supposed to be their nature. So the closing questions can be as aggressive as you can make them (within the context of the rest of the interview, of course, and with due respect for the personality of the interviewer):

I believe I've demonstrated the qualifications, experience, and attitude you're looking for. When can I start?

There's clearly a fit here. I'm ready to come aboard immediately and exceed your expectations. Can we discuss the details of my package?

I'm sure we'll have no trouble dealing with com-pensation issues. Can we start by discussing a salary slightly higher than you advertised?

These and similar questions that you should now be able to construct on your own have two things in common: They exude confidence, and they assume that the job is already won. The latter, naturally enough called an "assumptive close," is virtually de rigueur for any salesperson. But it is certainly a *way* for more aggressive interviewees of any stripe to "go for the close."

GETTING TO YES

Young salespeople are taught the importance of getting prospects to say "yes." Neophytes are often given a series of scripted, closed-ended questions to ask with the sole purpose of getting a series of "yes's," on the assumption that if someone says "yes" enough, they'll fall right into the "yes" that matters—"Do you want to buy my product/service?"

Without going into the plusses and minuses of such a sales technique, let me suggest that there is an adaptation that might be appropriate in some interviews or with some interviewers. Especially, it seems to me, those who haven't conducted the clearest interview of all time or who have given you the impression that they're a little lost. Perhaps you can help them toward a decision with this technique. I've created two sample scripts (below). Until the end, I'm going to assume you have done a wonderful job and the only thing the interviewer can say is, of course, "YES":

> *"Mr. Barnes, have we established that I have the educational background you're seeking?"*

> *"And do I have the breadth of experience you want?"*

> *"Have my answers allayed any concerns you may have had about my abilities?"*

> *"Am I someone you feel you and your team can comfortably work with?"*

Presuming a series of resounding "yes's" in response, the sales candidate would be ready to close:

> *"So, should we start discussing my compensation package and make arrangements to bring me on board?"*

Here's a more detailed way to get to the same place:

> *"Mr. Olsen, the original ad that brought us together detailed a number of qualifications. May I go over them briefly with you?"* (YES)

> *"I think it's important that we review what we've discussed and make sure I haven't failed to discuss an important topic, wouldn't you agree?"* (YES)

"The ad specified a BA degree from a four-year college, right?" (YES)

"An English major?" (YES)

"Coursework in creative writing?" (YES)

"An internship for at least two summers?" (YES)

"Two to three years of on-the-job experience in consumer magazine editing?" (YES)

"Some experience with layout?" (YES)

"It also stated that the company wanted a 'go-getter,' someone ready to move higher up in publishing and take over the reins of the entire magazine within five years." (YES)

"Obviously, these requirements are just the tip of the iceberg. You want an individual that will fit in with your corporate culture, someone your and my future coworkers will be able to get along with. Do you think I have the personality and personal style to do so?" (YES)

"Have I answered all of your questions satisfactorily?" (YES)

If at any point your questions elicit a "no," you would pause, clarify the misinformation, confirm that you now understood each other, then restate the question in a way that would restart the series of "yes's." Otherwise, you would immediately proceed to a series of closing questions:

Can I assume from your positive responses that I am a serious candidate for the job?

Can you tell me where you are in the process?

How many other candidates would you say you still believe have a shot at this job after talking to me today? (This is a strong close, but it's very positive, and I personally like it a lot)

Whom do I need to talk to next? May I set up an appointment with her before I leave today?

When do you expect to make a final decision and fill the position?

Frankly, even an aggressive sales type should avoid being *too* pushy. Pressuring an interviewer for a decision by a specific day (or, worse, immediately) may be going overboard at all but the most Type-A companies. However, if you acknowledge that you're *being* pushy, you may get away with it! For example,

> *"Mr. Barnes, I like you, I like the people I've met, I like the company, and I am excited about this opportunity. I don't mean to come on too strong, but I have been interviewing elsewhere and I am expecting at least _____ other offers before the end of the week. Is there any way I can hear from you before Friday?"*

The nicest thing about this question is that it makes you seem even more attractive: *"Hey,"* you're announcing, *"other companies are ready to make me an offer. What's wrong with you?"*

YOU CAN ALWAYS WORK FOR FREE

> *"I realize you have a very difficult decision to make, but since you've indicated you need at least a week to do so, would you object if I came in first thing tomorrow morning and actually showed you what I can do? I wouldn't expect payment, of course, until you officially hire me at the end of the week."*

Speaking as someone who has hired hundreds, and who still sometimes worries that I've missed *some*thing and may be making the wrong choice, it would be mighty hard for me to pass up this "free trial offer." It completely devastates the competition! It effectively puts off the decision for a week—a week during which *you* are in the office, working away, making friends, and influencing people, while your competitors are, what, sitting by their phones? You have taken control.

Do you really think the decision was being made in a week? Who cares anymore? You are in a position to force the decision to be made in a week. You have closed the presale and put yourself in an unbelievable position. Is there any question in your mind as to whether you'll be hired at the end of the week? Only if you really can't do the job, they hate you, or you hate them. In which case you've saved everyone a lot of grief and only "wasted" a week!

QUESTIONS TO ASK YOURSELF AFTER EVERY INTERVIEW

Kate Wendleton, founder and president of The Five O'clock Club, a national job-networking organization, has her counselors ask a series of questions of every candidate when they return from an interview. I heartily recommend that you ask yourself the same questions (and take notes on your answers):

How did it go?

What did they say?

What did you say?

How many people did you see?

How much time did you spend with each?

What role does each person play?

Who seemed the most important?

Who is the hiring manager?

Who is the decision maker?

Who seems to most influence the decision?

Who else did you meet (secretaries, receptionists, department heads, peers, etc.)?

How quickly do they want to make a decision?

How do you stack up to your competition?

What objections did you have to overcome? Do you think you did so successfully?

How badly do you want this job?

What's the next step according to them?

What is *your* plan?

7

Questions to Get the Best Deal

A sk a few experts about dealing with salary issues during an interview, and you'll undoubtedly receive a range of advice. Some experts advise bringing the topic to a head as soon as possible. Others suggest avoiding the subject entirely, as if getting a paycheck were some unspeakable practice, inquiring about that filthy lucre somehow too indelicate.

Common sense dictates a course somewhere between these two extremes. I recommend that you avoid bringing up the subject of salary yourself during your screening and selection interviews. If the interviewer brings it up, do your best to deflect her. It's really in your best interest to avoid getting down to the brass tacks of salary negotiation *until an offer has been made.* Not talking about salary at some point is, of course, ludicrous. But talking about it at the *wrong* time is just foolish.

So don't discuss dollars and cents until after you've convinced the interviewer that you're the best person for the job. Until you've made it over all the other interview hurdles, the interviewer is still assessing your ability. And he or she is probably still seeing other contenders as well, including some whose talents, unfortunately, may come cheaper than yours.

The interview is a classic buy-sell situation: You are trying to sell yourself to a company and get the best price you can. The company is making sure that it wants to buy what you're offering, and, if so, hopes to pay as little as you'll accept.

If you can stand apart from the crowd of applicants, if you can convince the employer that an extra couple of thousand dollars would be well-spent on a dynamo like you, then one of the only sure ways *not* to get it is by hanging a price tag around your neck too early in the proceedings.

If the interviewer is loathe to bring up salary during the early stages of an interview, then your bringing it up is a sure way to make him feel you are self-absorbed and interested solely in the money.

Would you buy something from a salesperson who only wanted to impress upon you how much something cost?

Of course not.

Why would a company hire someone only interested in seeing how much he could get?

I, and most experienced hiring managers I know, have at least one story about candidates who asked only about salary, benefits, and days off . . . just before they were thanked and shown the door. *None* of these subjects is one to raise when an employer asks, *"So, do you have any questions?"*

But even if an interviewer tries to pressure you into naming a specific number early in the game, avoid committing yourself. Instead, cite a very broad salary range. You might say, *"I believe a fair wage for this kind of position would be between $60,000 and $68,000."* The higher the salary, the broader the range you can name. (Be sure the bottom end of that range is no less than the minimum salary you would be willing to accept for the position.)

You should, of course, have a pretty good idea of what your particular market will bear long before you walk into the interview. If you don't know the pertinent salary ranges in your area (city and state) and industry, do some research. Make sure you know whether these figures represent just dollars or a compensation package that may include insurance, retirement programs, and other value-added benefits.

If you're a woman, make sure you know what men doing the same job are earning. You're bound to find a discrepancy, but you should request and expect to earn an equivalent salary, regardless of what women predecessors may have been paid.

It's important, so I'll say it again: Timing is everything. *You have nothing to gain by discussing dollars and cents before you've convinced the employer that you're the right person for the job. In other words, the best time to discuss salary is* after *you get the offer.*

WHAT IF THE INTERVIEWER BLINKS FIRST?

You can always tell when an interviewer is paying people too little: She will inevitably raise the salary issue early on to determine whether she can afford you before she wastes time interviewing you.

Okay, that might not always be the reason that the subject of salary is broached too early. It might just be that the interviewer is inexperienced or has a premonition that you'll want more than he can afford to pay.

Whatever the reason, if the subject of salary *does* come up too early, sidestep it. Remember: It can't possibly do you any good to discuss salary before you've sold the employer. One of the following replies might prove useful:

> *"I have an idea of the salary range for the position from your ad (or from what the recruiter said). It sounds like a reasonable range to me."*

"I'm willing to consider any reasonable salary offer."

"I'd feel more comfortable discussing salary after I understand my responsibilities better. Is that all right with you?"

"From what I know about the position and the company, I don't think we'll have any trouble agreeing on a fair salary."

"I'm aware of what salaries are for this position within the industry. I'm sure that if salaries here are comparable, we'll have no trouble coming to an agreement."

FIELDING THE OFFER

So, you're an ace candidate. You have impressed the interviewer so much that a couple of days later you get an offer by phone.

You're delirious. You want to shout with joy. You got the job!

Don't get too carried away just yet. You've captured the high ground in your search for a job. Now you want to take advantage of that strategic position.

Even if you've been out of a job for months, this is *not* the time or place to let your desperation show, so avoid gushing, *"Gee, this job sounds so gosh-darned wonderful I can't believe you're going to pay me anything! Just give me an office and a phone and I'll work for the sheer fun of it!"*

I stressed earlier that the interview is a buy-sell situation. Now that the company is sold on you, *you're* the one who must make the decision to buy.

Get the complete offer in writing, with all details spelled out. But be careful: I actually once interviewed someone who was so mistrustful she insisted that I confirm, in writing, that she be allowed to wear sneakers to the office every day . . . and that I had to notify her 24 hours in advance if I expected her to dress up for any reason. Otherwise, she intended to wear jeans in the winter and a T-shirt and shorts in the summer. And *that* had to be confirmed too.

Can you say, *"I'm sorry, I just changed my mind about hiring you?"* I did.

Take your time. You should never—repeat, *never*—accept a job the minute it's offered to you. Even though you've probably thought about little else since your last interview with the employer and have thoroughly made up your mind that you will accept the job if it *is* offered, politely inform the interviewer that you "need some time to consider it."

You could say you want to sleep on it, or think about it over the weekend, or talk it over with your spouse or "adviser."

Most companies will push you for a fairly quick response—they have probably interviewed other promising candidates for the position and don't want to lose *them* if you reject the offer.

However, don't act before *you're* ready to. Tell the person making the offer that you need a short time to think it over, thank her for thinking so highly of you, and agree on a day and time that you'll call back with your answer.

What's the first thing you should do once you've received an offer? *Tell all the other companies you've been interviewing with about it!* Much like the stock of a company that's perceived to be "in play," *your* perceived value to these companies will increase. Another interested company will know they can no longer sit on the fence about hiring you; it's either act now or forever lose you . . . perhaps to their competition.

That's another reason to ask the offering company for as long as possible to tell them your decision. You want to give all the other potential players time to get into the game!

QUESTIONS TO ASK WHEN YOU'VE GOTTEN AN OFFER

I'd like a little time to think about your generous offer. When would you like me to get back to you?

When would you like me to start (earliest or latest)?

If I have further questions, whom should I contact?

You indicated that my base pay would be _____, plus a bonus would be payable quarterly based on specific criteria you've outlined. I understand the medical benefits. You've also told me that I shouldn't expect consideration for a company car for one year. Are there any other items we need to discuss to make this offer complete?

Especially if the money isn't all you'd hoped for, you are looking for hints about how flexible the interviewer (or the company) can be about perks: Is a better title negotiable? Will they pay for your cell phone? Give you an advance against travel expenses? Reimburse your graduate school tuition? Buy you a laptop computer to use at work, at home, and on the road?

As I'll discuss a little later in this chapter, it is imperative that you consider the whole compensation package, not just the salary, when evaluating an offer.

WHAT TO DO IF YOU DON'T LIKE THEIR OFFER

You know the salary range for the job on offer. You either discovered it through your research, found out by asking a recruiter or Human Resources, or asked the hiring manager directly.

If you are offered a salary close to the top of that range, consider it a compliment and don't think too hard about pushing for more money. You don't have that much to gain anyway, particularly in today's performance-based job market.

But if you're offered a salary at the floor of the range, you may certainly consider making a case for a better deal. You may say something like:

> *"I understood that the position was paying as much as $84,000, and yet you're offering me only $77,500. You told me that you've interviewed several candidates for the position. Well, you've selected me because of my management and financial expertise, as well as my experience working with plastics. Therefore, I believe a salary of at least $81,000 is reasonable for me to expect."*

By *not* pushing for the very top of the range in this example, you have made it very easy for the interviewer to see it as a "win-win" situation and give you what amounts to an immediate $3,500 raise.

Never couple asking for more money with an explanation of why you need it. Rather, always couch such a request within a declaration of the "extra value" the employer should expect in return. Remind him of the cost savings and other benefits he'll enjoy when you come on board. For example, you might say:

> *"I was able to cut my previous employer's expenses 10 percent by negotiating better deals with vendors. I think it's reasonable to expect that any additional salary we agree on will be more than offset by the savings I will bring the company during my first few months on the job."*

If the interviewer won't budge and seems to have at least reasonably valid arguments as to why, ask when you will receive your first salary review. If the answer is on your anniversary date, see if you can push for an earlier review to make up some of the shortfall between the offer and your expectations:

> *"I am very flattered by the offer, though I wish we could have agreed on a slightly higher salary. Could you give me my first salary review in, say, 6 months, rather than 12?"*

This is a rather easy concession for the interviewer to make. He will think that he is getting you for only half the difference between what you want to earn and what he wants to pay.

Look for other win-win solutions. If the employer is adamant about not increasing your salary, he may be amenable to a company car or some other perk that works for both of you.

Unless you become overheated and frantic, employers expect negotiation. You will not lose the offer just because you try to negotiate—your willingness (or unwillingness) to do so may actually be the final test!

Even if you're disappointed, but have decided to take the job, make sure everything ends on a friendly note. Otherwise, you'll leave a bad impression and may be put under the microscope or on a short leash right from the start.

If you become too intransigent, you may even force them to change their minds! After all, you're already showing them you're not a team player by not giving an inch on anything, no matter how inconsequential.

THEY'RE OFFERING A PACKAGE, NOT JUST A SALARY

If you are already an experienced worker at any level, you are aware that salary is only part of the compensation package you can expect. But even if you are an entry-level candidate, I encourage you to analyze the entire value of the compensation package before making any decision. Some companies provide very generous benefits packages, including stock options, dental care, company cars, free lunches, and more, even to the rank and file. If these benefits don't fatten your take-home pay, at least you won't have to pay for them out of your own pocket.

Most company vacation policies are fairly standard—two weeks for the first three years, three weeks thereafter. Some companies offer "comp" time in exchange for overtime. Some match some or all employee donations to retirement plans. Some require employees to contribute something toward health insurance. A number of benefits, such as profit sharing, may only be available to senior-level employees.

You should have learned something about the company's standard benefits package early in the game. If, at this stage, you find the offer abysmal, why are you still considering that company?

If there are any other questions you feel will affect your decision about whether to accept this job, you had better ask them now, while you are still considering the offer!

Here's a comprehensive list of all forms of compensation, which, obviously, is far more extensive than just salary and a holiday bonus:

Basic compensation

Base salary

Deferred compensation (401(k), SEP-IRA, etc.)

Incentive compensation

    Performance bonus

    Sales commission

    Sales incentive plans

    Shares of stock

    Stock options/ESOPs

Matching investment programs

Medical insurance

Profit sharing

Signing bonus

Timing of first review

Perquisites

Accidental death insurance

Child/elder care allowance

"Comp" time

Commuting cost assistance/reimbursement

Company car or gas allowance

Continuing professional education

Conventions—paid attendance and expenses

Dental/vision insurance

Disability insurance (long- and/or short-term)

Employee assistance programs

Employee discounts

Executive dining room privileges

Executive office

Expense account

Extra sick/personal days

Extra vacation days or weeks

Financial planning assistance

First-class hotels or air travel

Furlough trips for overseas assignments

Lower contribution (or lower deductible) for medical coverage

Memberships

    Country club

    Luncheon club

    Athletic club

    Professional associations

Paid travel for spouse

Parking assistance/reimbursement

Personal use of frequent-flyer awards

Private secretary

Shorter waiting period to qualify for medical coverage

Tax assistance

Tuition assistance/reimbursement

Relocation expenses

Closing costs, bridge loan

Company purchase of your home

Discounted loans/mortgages

Home-buying trips

Lodging while between homes

Mortgage funds/short-term loans

Mortgage prepayment penalty

Mortgage rate differential/housing allowance

Moving expenses

Outplacement assistance for spouse

Real estate brokerage fees

Temporary dual housing

Trips home during dual housing

Related to severance

Consulting fees after termination

Insurance benefits after termination

Severance pay and outplacement, including extra weeks/months of severance

QUESTIONS TO ASK YOURSELF BEFORE SAYING "YES!"

Let's review some of the basic questions you asked yourself very early on (didn't you?): What's the purpose of your job hunt? To get an interview? Only if you enjoy collecting unemployment on the way to your next performance. To get a job? Well, sure, but what *kind* of job? How about getting a job that you will actually like, that you can actually do, that meshes with your values and interests, and offers future opportunities?

Don't get me wrong. There are certainly situations in which you can't be choosy—getting a job, *any* job, is preferable to cruising local trash bins. But those situations should be dire circumstances—if you don't get a job tomorrow, your family doesn't eat. Don't create those circumstances in your head and convince yourself that a job offer, any job offer, is something to leap at.

What good (again, except under the direst of circumstances) is getting a lousy job that you will wind up hating in a month . . . or less? Do you really want to restart this whole process from scratch? I didn't think so.

So as tempting as it is to accept an offer without a lot of deep analysis, especially if the money is exceptional (or, at least, more than you thought you were going to get), take the time to go through that analytical process and ask yourself these smart questions:

> **Do I really want this job?**
>
> **Does this job mesh with my long-term career plans, or is it an abrupt detour?**
>
> **Does the described career path mesh with my own?**
>
> **Can I really do this job as described? Will I enjoy doing it as described?**
>
> **Does the company's/department's culture match my strengths? Will I comfortably fit in with the team and/or department?**
>
> **Do I really like/respect the person I'll be working for?**
>
> **Do I like the people with whom I'll be working or whom I'll be managing?**
>
> **Is there anything else I need to know about *anything*—the company, department, job description, boss, team, subordinates, colleagues—to assure myself that this is the right move?**

And what's the purpose of asking questions? To get the job by showing how smart you are and how much research you've done? Only partly. Yep, that other part (and don't sell it short!) is to make sure the answers make you smile, not wince! A fast-paced environment where merit is quickly rewarded? Great! Just what you want, Ms. Type A. A cutthroat department where you'll need to spend half your time covering your ass and the other half sucking up? Don't think so, Ms. Nonprofit.

No matter how good the offer and how happy you are, don't think only of the present. Make sure you ask the following smart questions:

> **In this job or department, on what bases are raises and bonuses awarded?**

> **Could you tell me more about how bonuses are structured? How much is based on my individual performance? How much on the performance of the department/company/division/etc.?**

THE JOB DESCRIPTION IS NEGOTIABLE?

Remember that you are not just negotiating your compensation, you are also negotiating what particular work you will do for that salary (plus benefits and perks, of course). There is a lot more room to define a job the way *you* want than most employers will ever admit. The more they want you, the more flexible they may prove to be.

WHY DON'T YOU WANT ME?

Invariably (i.e., at least once in your lifetime!) you will not be offered a job, no matter how many times you've gone back, how many interviews you've had. There are many possible reasons. The job was more fluid than you thought—the company is rethinking its strategy and isn't even sure they're hiring anybody. Or they're redefining the job (which may or may not work in your favor). Or the executive who has to sign off on the decision went to the Bahamas . . . for three weeks. Or the hiring manager simply can't decide between you and another candidate. Or two. Or three.

There are two kinds of rejection that occur during the job-search process: the kind you expect and the kind you don't. The first is easy to understand and describe. I once interviewed for a vice-presidency at a prestigious international travel magazine. I knew things had not gotten off to a good start when I met the interviewer at a restaurant—he looked like he had just stepped out of the pages of GQ. And I . . . well, I didn't. I wasn't wearing jeans and I didn't have nose hairs creeping out of both nostrils, but I was clearly in a different sartorial league. I saw the evaluating look in his eyes and knew I had already taken my first strike. (As it turns out, it was probably three strikes right then and there. The person he hired was a lightweight salesperson and manager but a charming rake with a monstrous closet of designer duds.)

Within 15 minutes, I knew I had definitely struck out. In answer to a very specific question, I happily noted that I did indeed have the unusual experience he said he needed. Had done it for 6 months at a single job. There was then a long pause, as he unsuccessfully scanned my resume for any hint of that job . . . and I realized I would be leaving long before dessert.

My duplicitous attempt to "sanitize" my resume to avoid a charge of job-hopping was clearly not the smartest thing I had ever done.

And my lack of sartorial splendor, which clearly cost me the job before I had read the menu? It was an unstated but highly implied requirement for the job that I failed to even contemplate; I just didn't think of clothes as anything more than something you wore because society didn't condone running naked around the office. Not only would I never get a job where model-level grooming was a keenly desired trait, I would never *want* such a job.

The lesson learned was more subtle but far more important: Think about the real requirements for the job and make sure they match not just your desires but "you." If I had thought for even a moment, it should have been apparent that the audience for such a magazine would be decidedly upscale, as would the advertisers, as should the image of the salesperson trying to *sell* those advertisers. I work hard, work fast, and get great results. But I am not going to give anyone the impression that I am Ralph Lauren incarnate. Nor, if I want to have a happy life, should I try.

What if you believed in your soul that you knocked the interviewer's socks off? If it comes as a genuine shock that you didn't receive an offer at the top end of the salary range, let alone any offer at all? Go through your memory and your interview notes to see if you missed something. Did the interviewer hint that he had a problem with something that you simply ignored in your haste to talk about something else?

But be aware that there are many reasons this might have occurred, and certainly not all of them are even remotely connected to your interview. The job description may have changed without your knowledge. Another candidate with much stronger credentials may have waltzed in and delegated you to that sad "Strong Number Two" position. The position may not even have been available; the interviewer may have concocted a quick one- or two-day experiment to see if there was someone out there better than the employee he already had. (In my experience, this happens in smaller companies all the time, especially family-run firms.) You may not only have had to impress the interviewer more than the other candidates, but also beat out the guy already on the job!

Will you ever know for sure? Probably not. Not that long ago, I would have given you a bunch of advice on how to get the interviewer to give you some hints "so I can do better the next time." Unfortunately, the hiring landscape has changed pretty dramatically in the last couple of decades. Employers are so scared of being sued that it's difficult for another employer to get more than "name, rank, and serial number" (name, title, and salary) when calling for a new employee reference. Believe me—I'm the only person in my company who is allowed to talk to someone asking for a reference. And I say virtually nothing, certainly nothing even remotely negative. Which is, after all, why they've called me in the first place: to ensure they aren't hiring someone I just fired for embezzlement, sheer craziness, or killing my cats. Sorry, no other info. Good luck. Better you than me. Let the cats out . . . quick.

If you're working with a recruiter or headhunter, he or she may be in a position to get more information than you would on your own, but, again, don't count on it.

What if you left the interview with the distinct impression that there were unexpressed objections. You tried. You asked probing questions. You all but begged for feedback. Nada.

Then follow-up is even more important. If you know what the objection is, answer it in your follow-up letter. Then write another letter, raising the objection again and offering yet another reason why it isn't valid. And another.

The danger, of course, is that you're tilting at windmills of your own creation, that there *is* no real objection, just some of the above possibilities (vacation, indecision, etc.). In which case, all you're doing is drawing the interviewer's attention to some glaring hole in your resume or education or qualifications . . . which he never noticed before. But thanks to your input, you are now a noncandidate!

How do you follow up? Following an enthusiastic recounting of how much you want the job and how perfect your qualifications seem to mesh with their needs (either in a letter or during a telephone conversation), here are two smart questions to ask if a job offer doesn't materialize:

Is there more information I can give you?

I've been giving a lot of thought to (something you discussed) and have developed some (ideas, sketches, plans, proposals). May I come in and discuss them with you?

YOUR NEGOTIATING "CHEAT SHEET"

● **WAIT UNTIL YOU RECEIVE AN OFFER** before you discuss salary, benefits, vacation days, and the like. Deflect any question of salary that comes up early in the interview with an answer like this:

> *"From what I know about the position and the company, I don't think we'll have any trouble agreeing on a fair salary."*

or

> *"I'd like to know a little bit more about the job responsibilities and the level of expertise you're expecting before I feel comfortable discussing a salary."*

● **RESEARCH COMPENSATION LEVELS** within your industry, city, and state. If you don't already know the salary range for the specific position you're considering, find out. You need to go into salary negotiations armed with this information.

● **KNOW YOUR WORTH.** Once you receive a solid offer, you know that the company wants you. They have decided you are the best candidate they have met. This puts you in a position of power. If they balk at your initial salary demand, remind them of the specific benefits they stand to gain by hiring you.

● **GET IT IN WRITING.** Especially if you negotiate a complex, nonstandard salary/benefits package. Be sure you have something in writing—either a letter or memo from the employer or one you've sent that's been accepted—*before* you give notice to your current employer.

⬤ **NEGOTIATE THE PERKS.** Make sure you understand the value of *all* the potential benefits in the salary/benefits package. Benefits can vary widely and, depending on your level, could be a substantial part of your package.

⬤ **SHOOT FOR THE TOP SALARY.** If that is more than the company will pay, the interviewer will counter with another offer. Work toward a compromise from there. Employers expect some give-and-take. You will not make them angry if you remain calm and professional.

ONCE YOU'VE ACCEPTED AN OFFER

How do you convince someone who's just offered you a job that she absolutely made the right decision? Ask one of these smart questions:

Are there any upcoming events occurring before my start date in which I could participate?

The more social, the better. You really want to get to know your boss, peers, and subordinates once they've "let their hair down." (If they remain stiff and formal even at social events, there's a message there, too!) So a company picnic is great. A departmental Friday night "let's-have-a-beer-together" is nice, though socially tough if you're not a butterfly. It would be most beneficial if you could attend one of these before you make a decision, but that's unlikely. However, if there's a big press conference or similar corporate event, you could always ask to attend. A little exposure to the Big Wigs to see what they're really saying in public as opposed to what they told you during the interview may prove enlightening.

What could I do before my first day to jump-start my entry into the department?

Is there any reading I can do to prepare for my first day (reports, memos, whatever)?

Both of these (and similar) questions will confirm to the interviewer that he has made the right decision. Look at that passion! That interest! That aggression!

EPILOGUE

Questions That Get Real

In the Introduction, I boiled down 101 tough interview questions to 5. Well, I'm going to boil down the many smart questions I've suggested you ask to 6. When all is said and done, here's what you absolutely want to know before you accept any job:

Can I do the job?

Are you really qualified? Be honest with yourself, because if the answer is "no," sooner or later it will not be a secret to your boss!

Do I *want* to do the job?

They may love and want you, but you'd better be sure this is a job you can be passionate about. If not, but you plan to take it anyway, you should at least be honest and *know* you are compromising for a reason that is valid to you . . . like, you have to eat.

Does this job fit in with my long-range plans?

The more solid and thought-out your long-range goals, the easier it is to create a directed and targeted career *path* rather than simply a series of jobs that fail to build upon one another. Just as you can and should take charge of the interview, you must control your own career path. Make sure you have honestly analyzed whether this job fits in with your own goals.

Will I fit in?

Did you like your boss? Did you like the people you'll be working with? Those you'll be managing? A job is not simply a set of functions; it's a collection of environments created by all the other people that work at the company. You may be totally qualified for and challenged by the job itself, but if you can't stand any of the people, how long do you think you're going to last?

Can I live on what they want to pay me?

I've lectured you enough about keeping money in perspective, but one does have to live. If your ideal job won't even pay the rent or the mortgage, you have a problem. But the biggest problem is if you haven't bothered to think about your financial needs at all.

Do I feel secure taking a job at _____?

Doubling your salary may be wonderful. Stock options could make you rich. Or you could find yourself back on the street in a month if you haven't bothered to ask yourself this question. Always evaluate the compensation package in concert with your analysis of the health of the company. It doesn't matter how much they promise to pay you if they're heading towards bankruptcy.

APPENDIX 1

20 Great Answers to the Toughest Interview Questions

Employers are looking for self-managing employees—people who are versatile, confident, ready and able to work with a team, and not afraid to roll up their sleeves, work long hours, and get the job done. "That's me," you chortle. Congratulations. But you won't get the chance to prove yourself on the job without making it through the interview process.

Of all the tools in your professional arsenal, your ability to shine in one brief moment in time—your initial interview—can make or break your chances for a second go-around, and, ultimately, dictate whether you're ever given a shot at the job. I hope to spare you many of the indignities I suffered along the way, by helping you prepare for the interview of your worst nightmares—at a comfortable remove from the interviewer's glare.

1. So, tell me about yourself.

Construct a well-thought-out, logically sequenced summary of your experience, skills, talents, and schooling. But be sure to keep it tightly focused—about 250 to 350 words, chock-full of specifics—and tie your experience to the requirements of the position. It should take you no more than two or three minutes to recite an answer that features a brief introduction, key accomplishments, key strengths demonstrated by these accomplishments, the importance of these strengths to the prospective employer, and where and how you see yourself developing in the position for which you're applying.

2. What are your strengths as an employee?

Let's presume you have a singular skill for meeting even the most unreasonable deadlines. You are tenacious. Nothing can stop you. If meeting deadlines is a key job requirement, be sure to cite two or three pertinent examples from your experience. The more outrageous the deadline and Herculean your efforts, the more important it is to bring to the interviewer's attention—at least twice.

3. What do you want to be doing five years from now?

Naturally, you want a position of responsibility in your field. But you don't want to give the impression that you're a piranha waiting to feed on the guppies in your new department. So, start humbly and then toot your own horn a bit.

4. What does success mean to you?

You should offer a balanced answer to this question, citing personal as well as professional examples. If your successes are exclusively job-related, an interviewer may wonder if you actually have a life. However, if you blather on about your personal goals and accomplishments, you may seem uncommitted to striving for success on the job.

5. Why are you applying for a job in a field other than your major?

Life doesn't always turn out according to plan. Especially when you're young, changes in direction are common, though hard enough to live through without getting grilled about them. But when the interviewer asks about one of your 180-degree turns, you've got to respond. So what do you do? You know you've piqued the employer's interest enough to get an interview, right? So relax and answer the question. Keep it brief and positive: You've reexamined your career goals, and you've decided *this* is the career you want to pursue.

6. Tell me about your last three positions. Explain what you did, how you did it, the people you worked for, and the people you worked with.

This is a "shotgun approach" question, in part designed to see how well you organize what could be a lot of data into a brief, coherent overview of 3, 5, 10, or more years' experience. Interviewers who ask this question, or one like it, are trying to flesh out your resume, catch inconsistencies, create a road map for the far more detailed inquiries to follow, and evaluate how well you edit your answer to match your experience and skills to the requirements of the job at hand. Try to highlight relevant experience and skills in a brief, coherent, positive answer and indicate a clear pattern *upward:* increased responsibility, authority, money, subordinates, skill level, and so on.

7. Tell me about the best/worst boss you ever had.

Most companies want to hear that you most enjoyed working for someone who was interested in helping you learn and grow, involved in monitoring your progress, and generous about giving credit when and to whom it was due. This question offers you an opportunity to accentuate your own experiences, accomplishments, and qualities. There are bad bosses out there, but a savvy candidate should be able to put a supervisor's failures in a positive context. If you say your boss was "stingy with his knowledge," you are accentuating your desire to learn. In the same vein, saying that a manager was "uninvolved" could indicate your desire to work within a cohesive team. Just prepare—and practice—your responses ahead of time.

8. What were the most memorable accomplishments at your last job? In your career?

Focus on your most recent accomplishments—in your current position or the job you had just prior to this one. But make sure they are relevant to the position for which you're interviewing. By letting the interviewer know that you are in the practice of regularly assessing your shortcomings, you will show that you are well on the way to overcoming them.

9. Tell me about the types of people you have trouble getting along with.

This could be a land mine for a candidate who responds too quickly, saying "pushy, abrasive people" only to find out later that the interviewer is known for being brusque. A general, vague answer, supplying little detail, indicates both a lack of analysis and a dearth of self-knowledge. Of course, you don't really want to answer this question, which is why it was asked. Keep your answer short and sweet and discuss what you have done to solve the "problem."

10. How do you handle change?

Business is about change. In order to remain competitive, companies have to adapt to changes in technology, personnel, leadership, business structure, the types of services they deliver, and even the products they produce. And their people need to change just as quickly. Choose an example of a change you faced that's resulted in something positive. Try to show that you not only accepted change and adapted to it, but flourished.

11. Do you prefer to work by yourself or with others?

The position for which you're interviewing will dictate how you should shape your answer. Even if you do like interaction at work, don't try to paint your environment as a bed of roses without any thorns. You know the old saying, "You can choose your friends, but you can't choose your relatives." That goes for coworkers, too. Every job situation forces us to get along with people we might not choose to socialize with. But we must get along with them and, quite often, for long stretches of time and under difficult circumstances. Acknowledging this shows strength. Talk about how you've been able to get along with a variety of other people.

12. How do you generally handle conflict?

Discuss how you try to anticipate problems before they occur and work them out before they get ugly. When conflicts can't be avoided, you don't back down, but you certainly try to be reasonable.

13. How do you motivate people?

A good answer will note how it "depends on the person," then offer one or two concrete examples. A poor candidate will imply that all people are motivated by the same thing or can be motivated with the same approach, a kind of one-size-fits-all philosophy.

14. Tell me about the last time you found a creative solution to a problem.

This open-ended question encourages you to talk but clearly requires a focused, specific answer—the more detailed the better. Provide an answer that has a beginning, middle, and end, much like a good story: Here's what happened, here's what I did, here's what I learned. Take appropriate credit for an accomplishment (reducing costs, increasing revenues, a creative solution, a tough sale), but be fair and honest enough to put your own contribution within the context of what your team/organization/boss/assistants did . . . and try to appear to be bending over backwards to do so. Most interviewers will favor a candidate who has been around long enough to make good *and* bad decisions, good *and* bad hires, good and bad *choices.*

15. Why are you thinking of leaving your current job?

Obviously, no one wants to leave a job with which they are completely satisfied, but the last thing you want to do is appear negative or, worse, speak badly about your current employer. So handle your discontent (if that's what led you here) very gingerly. The greater your unhappiness, the more careful you should be when talking about it. It will do you absolutely no good to confess to the interviewer that you lie awake nights fantasizing about putting a contract out on your current boss. Instead, use what management consultants call "visioning": Imagine the ideal next step in your career, then act as though you are interviewing for that position.

16. How would your coworkers describe you?

Of course, they would describe you as an easy-going person who is a good team player. After all, you've found that "a lot more can be accomplished when people gang up on a problem rather than on each other." Take words describing your strongest skills, greatest areas of knowledge, and greatest personality strengths . . . and put them in the mouths of coworkers and friends.

17. Do you know much about our company?

Toss out a few salient (and positive) facts about the company, and finish by lobbing a question that demonstrates your interest back into the interviewer's court. Give a detailed answer that indicates the breadth of your research, from checking out the company's Internet site to reading its annual report and becoming familiar with its products and services. Referring to a trade magazine article that mentions the company or, better yet, the interviewer, would be a nice touch, don't you think?

18. What interests you most about this position? Our company?

You have your eye on more responsibility, more opportunities, the chance to supervise more people, and the chance to develop a new set of skills and sharpen the ones you've already acquired. And, of course, if they absolutely insist they'll increase your salary, well, you certainly wouldn't be negative and say no! However, this is also the ideal time to show what you know about this company and how the position for which you're interviewing can contribute to its success.

19. What sort of salary are you looking for?

You must have a pretty good idea of what your particular market will bear. If you don't know the high and low salary ranges in your area (city and state) and industry, do some research. Make sure you know whether these figures represent just dollars or a compensation package that may include insurance, retirement programs, and other value-added benefits. Even if you've been out of a job for months, this is not the time or place to let your desperation show. Have confidence in your own worth. By this time, you've worked hard to sell the interviewer on your value as a future employee. Don't undermine your own argument.

20. Do you have any questions?

Normally, this question occurs very near the conclusion of the interview. In fact, you may well assume that its appearance pretty much signals the end. Never, I repeat, never answer with a "no." How can you make one of the most important decisions of your life—whether to work for this company, at this job—without knowing more? Even if you think you're sold on the position and are clear on the responsibilities, you must speak up here. If you don't, the interviewer will assume you are uninterested. And that can be the kiss of death even at this late stage of the process.

APPENDIX 2

Smart Questions to Ask

ABOUT THE COMPANY

Are you currently planning any acquisitions? (p. 87)

Do you have a lot of employees working flextime or telecommuting? (p. 110)

How fast is the company growing? (p. 108)

How many employees work for the organization? (p. 87)

Is there anything else you feel it is vital I know about the company? (p. 117)

Please explain the company's organizational chart. (p. 88, p. 107)

What are the company's strengths and weakness? (p. 20)

What are your goals in the next few years? (p. 88)

What are your key markets? Are they growing? (p. 87)

What are your leading products or services? (p. 87)

What are your plans and prospects for growth and expansion? (p. 87)

What do you like best about this company? Why? (p. 88, p. 115)

What do you see as the key goals for the company during the next year? (p. 113)

What growth rate are you currently anticipating? Will this be accomplished internally or through acquisitions? (p. 87)

What has been your layoff history in the last five years? Do you anticipate any cutbacks in the near future and, if you do, how will they impact my department or position? (p. 87)

What have you enjoyed most about working here? (p. 115)

What have you liked least about working here? (p. 115)

What is your hiring philosophy? (p. 87)

What is your ranking within the industry? Does this represent a change from where it was a year or a few years ago? (p. 88, p. 108)

What is your share of each of your markets? (p. 87)

What major problems or challenges have you recently faced? How were they addressed? What results do you expect? (p. 87)

Which other companies serving your markets pose a serious threat? (p. 87)

Who owns the company? (p. 87)

Will you be entering any new markets in the next couple of years? Which ones and via what types of distribution channels? (p. 87)

ABOUT THE DEPARTMENT

Are there specific challenges you are facing right now? (p. 107)

Can you tell me about a successful project and how you managed it? (p. 20)

Can you tell me about some recent problems you've faced and how you (as a team) overcame them? (p. 20)

Could you explain the organizational structure of the department and its primary functions and responsibilities? (p. 88)

How is the department's performance measured? (p. 109)

How many people work exclusively in this department? (p. 88)

If you could change one thing about the way this department works, what would it be? (p. 20)

To whom does my boss report? (p. 88)

To whom will I be reporting? (p. 70, p. 88)

What are the department's specific objectives for the next three months? (p. 108)

What are the department's strengths and weaknesses? (p. 20)

What are this department's current goals and objectives? (p. 88)

What has the turnover been in this department in the last couple of years? (p. 111)

What was the last great challenge faced by the department? How did you and your team handle it? (p. 20)

What problems is this department facing? (p. 88)

What would you most like to see changed in this department? (p. 109)

With which other departments would I work most closely? (p. 88)

ABOUT THE JOB

Are there a lot of after-hours business events I will be expected to attend? (p. 110)

Are there other things you would like someone to do that are not considered "formal" parts of the job? (p. 117)

Are there plans for new products or services I need to know about? (p. 109)

Could you describe a typical day in this position? (p. 89)

Does this job usually lead to other positions in the company? Which ones? (p. 89)

How advanced/current is the hardware and software I will be expected to use? (p. 89)

How did this job become available? Was the previous person promoted? What is his or her new title? Was the previous person fired? Why? (p. 89)

How do you see me working with each of the department heads? (p. 109)

How do you see my role evolving in the first two years? (p. 113)

How has this job been performed in the past? (p. 113)

How long has this position been available? (p. 89)

How many hours a week do you expect your star employees to put in? (p. 111)

How many people will be reporting to me? (p. 89)

How much budgetary responsibility would I have? (p. 111)

How much day-to-day autonomy will I have? (p. 89)

How much travel should I expect to do in a typical month? (p. 110)

How will we work together to establish objectives and deadlines in the first months of this job? (p. 116)

How would my performance be measured? (p. 109)

Is a written job description available? (p. 88)

Is relocation an option, a possibility, or a requirement? (p. 89)

Is there no one from within the organization who is qualified for this position? (p. 89)

On what basis are raises and bonuses awarded? (p. 145)

Please tell me a little bit about the people with whom I'll be working most closely. (p. 89)

Please tell me more about your training programs. Do you offer reimbursement for job-related education? Time off? (p. 88)

What are three specific goals I should set for my first three months on the job? (p. 116)

What are three things that need immediate attention? (p. 117)

What do you think my biggest challenge will be? (p. 113)

What is the first problem I should tackle? (p. 117)

What's the one thing I can do right at this job to assure my success? (p. 117)

What is the one thing I should do during my first three months on the job? (p. 113)

What kind of training should I expect and for how long? (p. 88)

What kinds of decisions could I make without oversight? (p. 112)

What skills are in short supply here? (p. 117)

What will my days be like? (p. 107)

What would be the most logical areas for me to evolve into? (p. 113)

What would you like to be able to say about your new hire one year from now? (p. 112)

Where will I be working? May I see it? (p. 89)

Would I be able to speak with the person who held this job previously? (p. 89)

ABOUT THE PROCESS (INCLUDING "CLOSING" QUESTIONS)

Are there any specific areas in which you believe my qualifications are lacking? (p. 123)

Before you're able to reach a hiring decision, how many more interviews should I expect to go through and with whom? (p. 90)

Can I assume that I am a serious candidate for the job? (p. 128)

Can we discuss the details of my package? (p. 126)

Can you tell me where you are in the process? (p.128)

Do you have any concerns I haven't adequately addressed? (p. 124)

Do you have any reservations about my ability to do this job? (p. 123)

How am I doing? (p. 125)

How do I compare with the others you've interviewed for this position? (p. 123)

How many other candidates have you interviewed? How many more will you be interviewing before you expect to make a decision? (p. 89)

How many other people would you say are also serious candidates for this position? (p. 123)

How much time have you set aside for interviews before you make a final decision? (p. 121)

How will you weight your subordinates' input? (p. 109)

Is there anything else I can tell you that would help you make the decision to hire me? (p. 124)

Is there anything that is stopping you from offering me this job right now? (p. 122)

Is there more information I can give you? (p. 148)

Over what period of time will those other interviews take place? (p. 121)

What are the key criteria you're going to use to decide callbacks? (p. 125)

What are the next steps in the hiring process? (p.125)

What kind of feedback does your boss expect you to give him? (p. 110)

When can I expect to hear from you? (p. 124)

When can I start? (p. 126)

When do you expect to make a final decision and fill the position? (p. 129)

When may I meet some of my potential colleagues (or subordinates)? (p. 109)

Where do we go from here? (p. 124)

Whom do I need to talk to next? (p. 129)

With whom will I be meeting next (names and job titles)? (p. 90)

ABOUT UPCOMING INTERVIEWERS

ABOUT YOUR BOSS'S "STYLE"

What's your philosophy about "mistakes"? (p. 114)

When's the last time you got really angry at one of your subordinates? What was the cause? What did you do? (p. 114)

AFTER EVERY INTERVIEW

How badly do you want this job? (p. 131)

How did it go? (p. 130)

How do you stack up to your competition? (p. 131)

How many people did you see? (p. 130)

How much time did you spend with each? (p. 130)

How quickly do they want to make a decision? (p. 131)

What did they say? (p. 130)

What did you say? (p. 130)

What's the next step according to them? (p. 131)

What is your plan? (p. 131)

What objections did you have to overcome? Do you think you did so successfully? (p. 131)

What role does each person play? (p. 130)

Who else did you meet (secretaries, receptionists, department heads, peers, etc.)? (p. 131)

Who is the decision maker? (p. 131)

Who is the hiring manager? (p. 131)

Who seemed the most important? (p. 131)

Who seems to most influence the decision? (p. 131)

AFTER RECEIVING AN OFFER

Are there any other items we need to discuss to make this offer complete? (p. 137)

Are there any upcoming events occurring before my start date in which I could participate? (p. 150)

If I have further questions, whom should I contact? (p. 137)

Is there any reading I can do to prepare for my first day? (p. 151)

What could I do before I start to jump-start my entry into the department? (p. 151)

When would you like me to get back to you? (p. 137)

When would you like me to start? (p. 137)

AGENCIES AND RECRUITERS

Could I meet with some of the other people you've placed at this company? (p. 71)

Do you foresee any problems with the company meeting my financial needs? (p. 71)

How integral to the company's success is the department I'd be joining? (p. 72)

How long do you think the interview process for this job will take? (p. 71)

How long has this job been open? (p. 70)

How long have you been working with this company? (p. 69)

How many candidates has the interviewer already seen? (p. 70)

How many people have you placed at this company? (p. 70)

How many people would be reporting to me? (p. 70)

Is a written, detailed job description available? (p. 70)

Is the interviewer my potential boss? (p. 71)

Is the person with whom I'm interviewing the decision maker? (p. 71)

Is this a new position? Was it created as part of a new project, division, or strategy? (p. 70)

Tell me about the company. (p. 69)

To whom would I be reporting? (p. 70)

What can you tell me about the culture of the company? (p. 71)

What else do I need to know? (p. 72)

What happened to the person who previously held this position? (p. 70)

Who is your contact at the company? (p. 69)

Why is this job available? (p. 70)

BEFORE YOU ACCEPT AN OFFER

Can I really do this job as described? Will I enjoy doing it as described? (p. 144)

Do I like the people with whom I'll be working or whom I'll be managing? (p. 144)

Do I really like/respect the person I'll be working for? (p. 144)

Do I really want this job? (p. 144)

Does the company's/department's culture match my strengths? Will I comfortably fit in with the team and/or department? (p. 144)

Does the described "career path" mesh with my own? (p. 144)

Does this job mesh with my long-term career plans, or is it an abrupt detour? (p. 144)

DURING AN INFORMATIONAL INTERVIEW

Can you direct me to others at your organization whom you think I should meet? (p. 68)

Do you know anyone at the organizations I've targeted? (p. 68)

Given my credentials, where would you see me fitting in at a company such as yours? (p. 68)

How can I learn more about this field? (p. 67)

How can I meet others in this field? (p. 67)

How did you get started at this company (or in your profession)? (p. 67)

How do you spend your day? (p. 67)

What are your duties and responsibilities? (p. 67)

What do you like least about your job? (p. 67)

What do you like most about your job? (p. 67)

What is the best way to get started (in this field or at this company)? (p. 67)

What kind of person do you think is right for this kind of work? (p. 67)

What skills are in short supply here? (p. 67)

HUMAN RESOURCES

Are there any challenges facing this department right now? (p. 76)

Can you tell me more about what I'd be doing on a daily basis? (p. 75)

Do you have a written description of the position? (p. 76)

Do you have any concerns about my abilities? (p.75)

Does the company have a mission statement or written philosophy? (p. 76)

How quickly are you hoping to fill this position? (p. 75)

How would you characterize the company's overall management style? (p. 75)

How would you describe the corporate culture? (p. 75)

How would you say I stack up against the other candidates you've interviewed? (p. 75)

What are your recruiting plans this year? (p. 74)

What can you tell me about my boss? (p. 76)

What can you tell me about the interviewer? (p.76)

What can you tell me about the people I'll be managing? (p. 76)

What can you tell me about the people with whom I'll be working? (p. 76)

What's a key thing about your company you'd like potential new hires to know? (p. 74)

What other positions at the company should this job prepare me for? (p. 77)

Where are you in the decision-making process? (p. 75)

PEERS (FUTURE COLLEAGUES)

Do you consider this company to be an ideal employer? (p. 79)

Does the company support you with ongoing training and education? (p. 79)

How are your contributions to the organization measured? (p. 79)

How long have you worked for your manager? (p. 79)

How many hours a day do you usually work? Do you have to work weekends? (p. 79)

How would you characterize your manager's management style? (p. 79)

If you had to do it over again, would you work here? (p. 79)

What can you tell me about working for this company? (p. 79)

What do you consider this company's (department's) strengths and weaknesses? (p. 79)

What do you wish you had known before you took your job? (p. 79)

What were your expectations when you started here? Were they met? How have they changed? (p. 78)

Why did you decide to work here? (p. 78)

YOURSELF

Am I overqualified for this position? (p. 77)

Are you a good loser or a bad winner? (p. 30)

Are you a risk taker or risk averse? (p. 29)

Are you overly competitive? Do you give up too easily? (p. 30)

Can I live on what this company wants to pay me? (p. 45)

Can you achieve your ultimate career path in your current company? (p. 49)

Can you comfortably afford your current lifestyle? (p. 45)

Describe your personality. (p. 29)

Do I want to do the job? (p. 144)

Do you have the qualities generally associated with the level of responsibility/job title you are seeking? (p. 33)

Do you mind traveling frequently? (p. 36)

Do you rise to a challenge or back away? (p. 30)

Does this job fit in with my long-range plans? (p. 144)

How can you make yourself more marketable in today's competitive job market? (p. 31)

How can you transfer skills you already have to a completely different career? (p. 49)

How do your positive attributes match up with the qualities you believe are necessary for success in the job/career path you've chosen? (p. 33)

How does your current job differ from your ideal job? (p. 49)

How does your self-description match that of the culture at the company you're considering? (p. 42)

How many of your positive qualities do you want to use in your job? (p. 34)

How much time are you willing to devote to a daily commute? (p. 36)

How well do you interact with authority figures? (p. 37)

How would you describe your dream job? (p. 49)

If you had to spend 40 hours a week doing a single activity, what would it be? (p. 30)

If you were to ask a group of friends and acquaintances to describe you, what adjectives would they use? (p. 30)

In what size city do you want to work? (p. 36)

In what size company do you want to work? (p. 28)

Is a formal employee-training program important to you? (p. 37)

Is a tuition reimbursement plan important to you? (p. 37)

What activities do you least like doing? (p. 29)

What activities do you most like doing? (p. 29)

What additional education or training would you need to achieve your dream job? (p. 49)

What are your goals and aspirations? (p. 31)

What are your key values? (p. 29)

What are your long-term goals? (p. 28)

What are your passions? (p. 31)

What are your short-term goals? (p. 28)

What are your strengths? (p. 28)

What benefits do you require? (p. 37)

What can you learn from past bosses? (p. 37)

What games and sports do you enjoy? (p. 30)

What has caused you to break up friendships? (p.30)

What have you already done to accomplish your short-term goals? (p. 28)

What in your personal life causes you the most stress? (p. 29)

What in your personal life gives you the most pleasure? (p. 30)

What is important to you? (p. 28)

What's the lowest salary you'll accept? (p. 37)

What is your current standard of living, and are you happy with it? (p. 45)

What kinds do you dislike working with? (p. 30)

What kinds of friends do you tend to have? (p. 30)

What kinds of people do you enjoy spending time with? (p. 29)

What kinds of people do you like working with? (p. 30)

What kinds of products/services/accounts would you prefer to work with? (p. 36)

What salary would you like to receive? (p. 36)

What specific things do you require in the job you're seeking? (p. 28)

What standard of living do you aspire to in 2 years? 5 years? 10? (p. 45)

What were your favorite subjects in school? (p. 30)

What would it take to transform yourself into someone who's passionate about every workday? (p. 31)

Where (geographically) do you want to work? (p. 28, p. 36)

Who are you? (p. 28)

INDEX

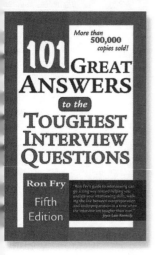

Best-selling author Ron Fry's 101 Series shows savvy job seekers how to turn even the most challenging job interviews into opportunities. Each book has been updated and revised to include more in-depth coverage of the interview process, various kinds of interviews job seekers may encounter, and tips for preparing and sending electronic job applications.

101 Great Answers to the Toughest Interview Questions, 5E
224 pp., 5 1/2" x 8 1/2", softcover, 2007
ISBN: 1-4180-4000-2 • List Price: $11.99 Z

Prepare for the trickiest questions with *101 Great Answers to the Toughest Interview Questions*, designed to help you pinpoint exactly what employers are asking and what they want to hear.

K E Y   F E A T U R E S

- Top tips from best selling career author, to get in the door and make the most of every interview
- Eye-catching series layout and design directs readers to key information and invites browsing
- Forms and checklists for preparing and organizing skills and experience

SOURCE CODE: FCCSFAP046A